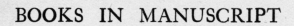

BOOKS IN MANUSCRIPT

PLATE I : BOOK OF KELLS (7th Cent., Irish).

Books in Manuscript

A Short Introduction
to their Study and Use.
With eight Illustrations.

By Falconer Madan, M.A.

Hon. Fellow of Brasenose College
Late Lecturer in Mediæval Palæography
in the University of Oxford

Second Edition, revised.

London
Kegan Paul, Trench, Trubner & Co., Ltd.
MCMXX

First Edition, 1893.
Second edition revised and corrected, 1920.

Preface

THE study of Manuscripts has a peculiar fascination for that fortunate minority of literary workers who have to do with them. There may be much to attract us in the external beauty of the writing or ornamentation. Their contents also, being often unpublished matter, may be fresh and stimulating objects of original research. But there is this special point about a manuscript, that any one is unlike every other, is unique, has a distinct individuality of its own. A written record, which is handing down the ages some literary treasure, does invest itself with a special colour and complexion, we may say, derived partly from the place and time and circumstances of its production, and partly from the personality of the man who wrote it. If we treat a manuscript as Henry Bradshaw treated a printed book, studying its peculiarities, making friends with it, and watching its features, as a portrait-painter his living subject, it will at length take us into its confidence, and will seem, as Ruskin said of the Alps, to " mutter and whisper to us garrulously, in broken and dreaming fits, as it were, about its childhood."

The present elementary work is intended to be a plain account of the study and use of manuscripts, such as may interest both the amateur who possesses manuscript treasures, but lacks the time or opportunity to go deeply into the subject, and the student who may wish to have a first view of the character and methods of the study, before entering on the endless details of palæography and textual criticism. There is little room for original matter, or for references to substantiate the statements made ; but the writer has attempted to be clear and readable, and to avoid exaggeration and prolixity. If the book leads collectors of manuscripts, or students either of the classics or of historical records, to take a keener and more intelligent interest in their work, its object will be attained.

F. MADAN.

Oxford, May, 1920.

Contents

PAGE

CHAPTER I

INTRODUCTORY, ... 1

CHAPTER II

MATERIALS FOR WRITING, AND FORMS OF BOOKS, . 6

CHAPTER III

THE HISTORY OF WRITING, ... 19

CHAPTER IV

SCRIBES AND THEIR WAYS, ... 40

CHAPTER V

ILLUMINATIONS, ... 55

CHAPTER VI

THE ERRORS OF SCRIBES AND THEIR CORRECTION, . 68

CHAPTER VII

FAMOUS LIBRARIES, ... 88

CHAPTER VIII

FAMOUS MANUSCRIPTS, ... 106

PAGE

CHAPTER IX

LITERARY FORGERIES, ... 127

CHAPTER X

TREATMENT AND CATALOGUING OF MANUSCRIPTS, . 153

CHAPTER XI

PUBLIC AND PRIVATE RECORDS, ... 167

APPENDIX A (STATISTICS OF PUBLIC COLLECTIONS OF MSS.) 181

APPENDIX B (CATALOGUES OF MSS. IN THE BRITISH MUSEUM, BODLEIAN, &C.), ... 184

APPENDIX C (SELECT BIBLIOGRAPHY), . . . 195

INDEX, ... 204

Illustrations

PLATE

I. BOOK OF KELLS (EARLY IRISH ILLUMINATION) *Frontispiece*

II. ST. MARK (PAGE FROM THE BEDFORD *Hours*) *opposite page* 1

III. SACRAMENTARY (CAROLINGIAN MINUSCULE
AND EARLIER HANDS) - - - - ,, 31

IV. SCRIPTORIUM (15TH CENT. SCRIBE AT WORK) ,, 45

V. APOCALYPSE (13TH CENT. FRENCH OR ENGLISH
SCRIPT AND MINIATURE) - - - - ,, 64

VI. ST. MICHAEL (PAGE FROM A FRENCH *Hours*) ,, 66

VII. SEND INSCRIPTION (EGYPTIAN HIEROGLYPHICS) ,, 106

VIII. CAEDMON (OLD ENGLISH SCRIPT AND
ILLUMINATION - - - - - - ,, 121

(*For notes on the above, see pp. xi.-xv.*)

NOTES ON ILLUSTRATIONS
(See p. ix.)
PLATE I. (BOOK OF KELLS).

Trinity College, Dublin, MS. (Book of Kells), fol. 290 (written in the second half of the seventh century in Ireland). *Front.*

A reproduction, by collotype, of Plate IX. in J. O. Westwood's *Facsimiles of Miniatures of Anglo-Saxon and Irish Manuscripts*, London, 1868, reduced about one-half in linear size. It represents the symbols of the four Evangelists, set in a framework of intricate geometrical design. The interlaced bands and spirals are deserving of minute examination, while the comparative rudeness of the drawings of living figures shows clearly the limitations of excellence in the Irish School (see pp. 61, 114). The principal colours are yellow, red, pink, and green. Some lacertine figures can be distinguished in two of the limbs of the large diagonal cross.

PLATE II. (ST. MARK).

Brit. Mus. MS., Add. 18,850, fol. 24 (the Bedford Hours). Written about A.D. 1425 in France. A collotype reproduction, reduced about one-half in linear size. *p. 1.*

The Bedford Hours (Horae B. Mariae Virginis) generally known as the Bedford Missal, one of the most splendid examples of fifteenth-century illumination, is a MS. written and painted for John, Duke of Bedford, son of Henry IV., and Anne, his wife, daughter of the Duke of Burgundy, after their marriage in 1423, and before the presentation of the volume to Henry VI. in 1430. The style is French, probably Burgundian ; and the illuminations are among the finest known. That in the plate represents St. Mark, ' comment Saint Marc escript l'Euuangile et a figure du lion.'' The lion, one wing of which is red and the other white, is depicted as holding the inkpot, and the Saint's left hand holds a blunt instrument for steadying the parchment, and preventing the contact of hand and sheet : by the side is a hanging lamp. There is appreciation of perspective in the drawing of the architectural background. The border represents scenes in the life of St. Mark. The first two lines run :—*In illo tempore accum* | *bentibus undecim disci.* The devolution of this volume has been remarkable :—The Duchess of Bedford presented it to Henry VI. ; but we find it next in the possession of Henry II. of France. After an interval of oblivion, it was purchased from Sir Robert Worsley's widow, early in the eighteenth century, by Edward Harley, second Earl of Oxford, from whom it passed to his daughter, the Duchess of Portland ; then it was successively sold, in 1786 to Mr. Edwards, a bookseller, in 1815 to the Duke of Marlborough, and in 1833 to Sir John Tobin, whose son disposed of it to the bookseller from whom the British Museum purchased it in 1852, thus placing it once more with the Harleian Collection.

PLATE III. (SACRAMENTARY).

Bodl. MS. Auct. D. 1. 20, fol. 120, lower part. (Written in the ninth century at Mainz.) *p.* 31.

An example (reproduced by photo-lithography) of ninth-century Continental writing and ornamentation, containing part of the Mass on the occasion of the dedication of a church of St. Michael. The first five lines are :—*Sanctorum, per dominum nostrum. III Kalendas Octobres id est XX.* | *VIIII die mensis Septembris. dedicatio basilice sancti angeli michaelis* | *Deus qui miro* | *ordine angelorum* | *mysteria hominumque dispensas.* | A fair representation of square capital (see page 27) is given by line 3 ; of Rustic Capitals (see page 27) in lines 1, 2, and 9 ; of uncial (see page 27) by line 4 ; and of ninth-century Carolingian minuscule by the rest (see page 28). The contracted style of Rustic capitals is well shown, and the rounded character of the ordinary hand, as opposed to the angular Gothic hand which followed it.

PLATE IV. (SCRIBE AT WORK).

Paris (National Library) MS., Fonds français 9,198, fol. 19. (Written in 1456, at the Hague, by Jean Mielot, secretary to Philip the Good, Duke of Burgundy.) *p.* 45.

This is a representation of Jean Mielot himself, writing his collection of Miracles of Our Lady in French, reproduced in collotype (by permission) from the collotype which is given in Sir G. F. Warner's *Miracles de Nostre Dame*, 1885, but reduced to about one-half the linear size. The scribe is writing on a large roll of parchment held steady by a weight, and holds in his left hand a knife for erasure (?), or possibly an instrument to keep the parchment firm without the contact of the hand. Above, on a separate desk, is the MS. to be copied, and by the side are three ink-bottles, while paint-pots hang on the wall. On the spectator's right is an *armarium*, or cupboard, holding other manuscripts, the upper part of which displays drawers which contain books, pens, and, apparently, a double eye-glass for purposes of close inspection. The volumes lying about afford good illustrations of binding.

PLATE V. (APOCALYPSE).

Bodl. MS. Douce 180, p. 61. (Written about A.D. 1280, probably in France.) *p.* 64.

The MS. contains the Apocalypse, with a commentary in Latin, and is reproduced by photo-lithography, reduced to about one-half the linear size of the original.

Illumination.—The subject is the delivery of the Seven Vials to the Seven Angels by one of the Four Beasts (Rev. xv. 5-7): the door of the Temple is represented in the background. It is in outline only, without colour, but the faces and general style are French or Anglo-Norman.

Writing.—The Gothic angular character, which came in in the thirteenth century (see page 30). The first three lines of the text and commentary are :—(1) *Et unus ex quatuor anima | libus dedit septem angelis | septem phialas aureas plenas :* (2) *Quatuor animalia quamuis quatuor euangelis | tas significent. tamen & simul & singulatim christum sig | nificent. Set quia breuitas non permittit ut dicamus.* The contrast between the rounded Carolingian minuscule and this set of letters, which are chiefly composed of straight lines, is well marked. It is probably French writing, but possibly, as accidentally left on the Plate itself, English.

PLATE VI. (St. Michael).

Bodl. ms. Douce 144, fol. 129ᵉ. (Written in A.D. 1407 in the Diocese of Paris.)   *p.* 66.

Illumination.—This plate, a collotype, reduced by about one-fourth in linear size, from a Book of Hours, represents St. Michael the Archangel slaying the Dragon. The inner margin is of a florid formal style, and rather in fourteenth-century style : the outer one is ' ivy-leaf ' work, and contains a representation of a soul weighed in the balance, and in the lower part a grotesque. The diaper background is also rather of the fourteenth than the fifteenth century in style. The colours are chiefly red, blue, and gold ; St. Michael's mantle is red, but inside, green ; his wings, green and yellow ; his armour, a steely blue : the red and blue diapers contain a ' fleur-de-lys ' : all the gold is of course burnished.

Writing.—*Michael archangele ueni in ad | iutorium populo dei. Verset. | In conspectu angelorum psallam | tibi deus meus. Respons.*—This is the beginning of the special service for St. Michael, often found in a Book of Hours, giving the introductory sentence, the Versicle, and the rubric of the Respond ; the rubrics being in French.

PLATE VII. (Send Inscription).

A photo-lithograph from the engraving in Lepsius's *Auswahl,* the size of the original monument being 1 ft. 6½ in. × 3 ft. 7½ in.   *p.* 106.

The following description is abbreviated from G. J. Chester's *Catalogue of the Egyptian Antiquities in the Ashmolean Museum, Oxford* (1881), page 47 :—A limestone cornice of the false door of a tomb on which, on the left, is a seated figure of S'era, a royal relative, a priest of Sent, king of the second dynasty. At the opposite side is the seated figure of Xenttek, a female, called Mare'st, an unknown title. Between them is a table, covered with reeds, on which is meat. At each end is a basin and water-jug. Above and below the hieroglyphs mention

incense, dates, wine, loaves, linen, flesh, etc., all offerings to
the king. ' This is, perhaps, the earliest Egyptian sculpture
known.' At present (1920) the probable date is about B.C. 3000.

The cartouche in the centre of the upper line contains the

king's name, thus $\left(\begin{smallmatrix} N \\ D \end{smallmatrix}\ S\right)$ = Send, alphabetically written (!)

and the N and D (see page 24) are the symbols which eventually
became our corresponding letters.

PLATE VIII. (CAEDMON).
Bodl. MS., Junius 11, p. 66. (Written about A.D. 1000 in a West-Saxon hand : reduced to about one-half the linear size.) *p.* 121.

Illumination.—The Ark, with animals on board : the type
of vessel appears to be Norse. The drapery, postures, and
faces are distinctively Old English. The side-rudder, dragon-
shaped boat, ornamental iron hinges, and architectural details
of the erection on deck are noticeable, and the expression on the
pilot's face. That the figure of Christ should be introduced is
a characteristic anachronism.

Writing (first three lines).—*Noe freme. swa hine nergend
heht. hyrde tham hal | gan. heofon cyninge ongan. ofostlice thæt
hof wyrcan. | micle mere cieste. magum sægde. thæt wæs threalic
thing.* | The style is pointed Old English, and characteristic
Hiberno-Saxon forms of letters are the *g*, *f*, and *r* : observe also
the high *e*, and the Old English letters, *th* (thorn) and *w* (wen),
as well as the barred *ð* in line 4 and elsewhere.

PLATE II : St. MARK. From the Bedford Hours, c. 1425.

BOOKS IN MANUSCRIPT

CHAPTER I

INTRODUCTORY

THE word 'Manuscript' (often written MS., in plural MSS.) is derived directly from the Latin expression *codices manu scripti* (books written by hand), and has always implied precisely what is indicated by its derivation. It is distinguished on the one hand from printed books (*codices impressi*, *libri impressi*), and on the other hand from kinds of record not naturally described as handwriting, such as inscriptions cut in stone and metal and wood, or stamped work like coins.

We, who are accustomed to a profusion of printed books on all possible subjects, may be tempted to consider the study of written records to be superfluous, and this first natural tendency is furthered by the undoubted fact that the manuscripts met with in our ordinary life are the most ephemeral of all the literature presented to us, largely consisting of private records of no permanent value, such as correspondence, diaries, or notes. Even in matters of law, where the importance of ancient records as

B

establishing or refuting a claim cannot be over-
looked, the tendency of modern legislation is to
make possession even more than ' nine-tenths of the
law,' and to bar all claims which have not been
recently asserted. Similarly, the modern politician
finds little to incite him to a study of palæography,
and trusts to the printing-press to supply him with
material.

But a student cannot too clearly set before
himself the simple fact that, until four and a half
centuries ago (A.D. 1440, say), *every record was a
written one*. Every monument of literature, every
treatise of philosophy, every historical chronicle,
every sacred writing which is older than the fifteenth
century,—whether preserved to us by the thinnest
possible thread of transmission, as are Tacitus and
Catullus and Beowulf, or by a body of evidence such
as that which supports the New Testament or Virgil,
—all this has come down to us solely and singly by
the vehicle of thought which is the special subject of
this book. For centuries such works were exposed
to all the chances and imperfections which attend
the scribe and his pen and his book, and, in the light
of modern discoveries connected with writing, we
can never safely claim that a printed edition
supersedes further study and comparison of the
manuscripts on which it is based.

And there is another reason why the study of
manuscripts is never likely to be a mere antiquarian
pursuit. When modern books on past history

written in the current style of literature and in the language of the day, are taken in hand, the student naturally finds very considerable difficulty in realising the actual surroundings of the time described. It is inevitable that to some extent this should be so ; but historians now endeavour to minimize it, by presenting in or side by side with their narrative, selections of original documents. These are wonderful helps to appreciation of the time, left in their old spelling and phraseology and appearance. It is to the same feeling that we owe the growing practice of profusely illustrating books. But a manuscript before one is more than all this, as every reader in the Public Record Office and every possessor of old historical records know. A despatch from Cromwell, hastily written during some campaign, an order from Charles I. marked ' for the printer,' but set aside in consequence of a hurried departure, bring the scene better before us than any laboured description, and there is a freshness in dealing with such records which no modern book, even with the powerful aid of photography, can supply. The terrible neglect of manuscripts in the past—whether historical, liturgical, or literary—shows how long we have taken to learn this lesson.

And once more, modern readers who are accustomed to skim the *Times* every morning and a novel every few days, when set down before some important historical work, find that their minds are as it were unstrung and incapable of close attention and

sustained effort. They are tempted to glance
superficially through volumes which ought to be
impressed on the mind, and they profit little by the
process. For these and such as these the study of
an original document in manuscript, a court-roll, a
charter, a page of a chronicle, an old political poem,
is the one corrective which suits the disease,—a
bracing, invigorating, and, it may be added, an
attractive exercise, the contact of Antæus with his
mother earth.

A caution may be here given. A student who
may be attracted to original work in mediæval or
ancient subjects can hardly even start unless he has
a sound knowledge of Latin. Latin was throughout
the Middle Ages the language of the Church, and the
lingua franca of scholars and historians and lawyers.
It is a *sine quâ non* for any serious study of mediæval
problems.

The aim of this little book is to familiarize the
possessor of a private collection of MSS., or one who
is about to enter on the study of them, with some
salient features of ancient writing ; with the forms
and kinds of books, and the conditions under which
they were produced and illustrated ; and with some of
the principles by which the errors of a copyist are
corrected. It will be lighter work to add a brief
account of some famous public and private collections, and of the vicissitudes and romances of a few
particular volumes. Finally, the proper treatment
and cataloguing of such books will also deserve

attention ; and a list of the more useful works
already produced on the subjects treated, with some
notices of libraries and their catalogues, will form a
natural appendix.

CHAPTER II

A.—*Materials*

PROBABLY the earliest efforts of the human race to record its thoughts and history were by scratching with some hard instrument on stone or bone. The permanence of the result has always made stone or metal a satisfactory substance to receive engraving, whether for sepulchral tablets, for some official records, such as State decrees, or for honorary inscriptions. Among obvious examples are the drawings of prehistoric man on the walls of caves, the Ten Commandments graven on stone, the Nicene Creed cut in silver by Pope Leo III.'s order (to fix the absolute form decreed by the second General Council), the Parian Chronicle, the Rosetta Stone, and tombs of all ages. It is on stone almost alone that we find in the early classical days of Rome the pure capital forms of letters, as on the tombs of the Scipios. And as material tends to act on style, and as curves are harder to grave than straight lines, writing on stone tends to discard the former and to encourage the latter, so that we find in such inscriptions a decided preference for angular forms of letters.

6

But another very early material for writing was the wood or bark of trees. It was easy to obtain, soft, and fairly durable. Three of our common terms are derived from the custom of cutting or scratching on wooden boards or bark, the Latin *liber* (a book, properly the bark of a tree, whence such words as *library, libretto*), the Latin *codex* (or *caudex*, a tree-stump, then sawn boards, then a book, now narrowed to a manuscript book ; compare *codicil*, a diminutive form), and perhaps the Teutonic word which appears in German as *Buch* and in English as *book*, meaning originally a beech tree and beechen boards.

Next we come to the substance which has given us much of the terminology of books. A common reed, chiefly found in Egypt, and known to the Greeks as πάπυρος (*papūros*), and to the Romans as *papyrus*, was discovered to be, when properly prepared, a facile and cheap material for writing. The inner rind was cut lengthways into thin strips (βύβλοι, *bubloi*), and laid in order thus :— On this was glued, with the help of rich Nile water or other substance, another set of slips laid on the former transversely, thus : This cross-formed substance, properly pressed, hammered and dried, presented a smooth but soft receptive surface for ink, and was most extensively used in classical times until parchment competed with it, or, more accurately, till the export of papyrus began to fail. The papyrus,

however, was not used in the form of our books, but
as a long roll, with the writing in broad columns
placed thus, the writing being represented by wavy
lines :—

Birt, in his book *Das antike Buchwesen* (1882), has
endeavoured to prove that there was a normal
length of about thirty-eight letters in each line, but
the length of the entire roll might be anything up to
150 feet.   There are also a face and a back to papyri,
a right and a wrong side for writing.   In the British
Museum there is a papyrus roll containing, in Greek,
the funeral oration of Hyperides on Leosthenes,
B.C. 323 ; on the other side of this is a horoscope of
a person born in A.D. 95.   Naturally, for some time
it was believed that the horoscope was casually
inscribed on the back of the Hyperides ; but a closer
examination has proved that the horoscope is on the
face of the papyrus, and the Hyperides perhaps a
school exercise accidentally entered on the back.
So that A.D. 95 is not the *terminus ad quem* of the
date, but the *terminus a quo*.

Unfortunately, of all possible materials for permanent record, papyrus is among the worst.   Even
when first written on, it must have seemed ominous

that a heavy stroke was wont to pierce and scratch the smooth surface; so much so that in all papyrus records the writing is along the line of the uppermost layers or strips (not across them), and is also of necessity light, and hardly distinguishable into up and down strokes. This foreshadowed the time when, on the complete drying of the substance in course of years, the residuum would be fragile, friable, and almost as brittle as dead leaves. Every papyrus that comes into a library should therefore be at once placed between two sheets of glass, to prevent, as far as possible, any further disintegration.

The terms used in connexion with writing in Greek, Latin and English are chiefly derived from the rolls of papyrus. Let us begin with two words which have had an interesting history. Our 'paper' is derived from the Greek πάπυρος (through the Latin *papyrus*), explained above as the name of an Egyptian reed. Thence it came to mean the papyrus as prepared to receive writing. How then has *paper*, which has always been made out of rags, usurped the name without taking over the material? Simply because the term came to signify whatever substance was commonly employed for writing; so when papyrus was disused (the latest date of its systematic use is the eleventh century), a material formed of rags was beginning to be known, and carried on, so to speak, the term. The Latin *charta* (paper) has had a partly similar history, for when first found it is applied to papyrus as distinguished from parchment.

Still more interesting is the word *Bible*. Βύβλοι (bubloi) was the Greek term for the strips of the inner part of papyrus. Then the book formed of papyrus began to be called βίβλος (*biblos*) and βιβλίον (*biblion*, a diminutive form). The Romans took over the second word, but chiefly used it in the plural, *biblia*, which came later to be regarded as a feminine singular, as if its genitive were *bibliæ* and not *bibliorum*. Lastly, the word became specially and exclusively applied to The Book, the Bible, and as such has passed into English. Other terms which recall the days of papyrus are *volume* (Latin *volumen*, ' a thing rolled up,' from *volvo*, I roll ; corresponding to the Greek κύλινδρος, *kulindros*), the long stretch of papyrus rolled up for putting away ; the Latin term *evolvere*, to unroll, in the sense of ' to read ' a book ; and the common word *explicit*, equivalent to ' the end,' but properly meaning ' *unrolled* ' (' *explicitus* '), the end of the roll having been reached.[1] So, too, the custom of writing on parchment with three or even four columns to a single page, as may be seen in our most ancient Greek MSS. of the New Testament, is probably a survival of the parallel columns of writing found on papyri.

We next come to the most satisfactory material ever discovered for purposes of writing and illumination, tough enough for preservation to immemorial

---

[1] It will be observed that ' explicit ' is a *vox nihili*, and can only be properly explained as a contraction of ' *explicit(us)* ' est liber, the book ' is *unrolled* to the end.' The corresponding term is *incipit*, ' here begins,' which is a good Latin word.

time, hard enough to bear thick strokes of pen or brush without the surface giving way, and yet fine enough for the most delicate ornamentation. *Parchment* is the prepared skin of animals, especially of the sheep and calf ; the finer quality derived from the calf being properly *vellum*, and if from the skin of an abortive calf, uterine vellum, the whitest and thinnest kind known, employed chiefly for elaborate miniatures. Parchment has neither the fragile surface of papyrus nor the coarseness of mediæval paper, and has therefore long enjoyed the favour of writers. Its only disadvantages in mediæval times were its comparative costliness and its thickness and weight, but neither of these was a formidable obstacle to its use. The name of this substance contains its history. In the first half of the second century before Christ, Eumenes II., King of Pergamum, found himself debarred, through some jealousy of the Ptolemies, from obtaining a sufficient supply of papyrus from Egypt. From necessity he had recourse to an ancient custom of preparing skins for the reception of writing by washing, dressing and rubbing them smooth ; probably adding some new appliances, by which his process became so famous that the material itself was called Περγαμηνή ; in Latin, *Pergamena*, ' stuff prepared at Pergamum,' whence the English word *parchment*. Both parchment and paper have had less effect than stone or papyrus on styles of writing, because both are adapted to receive almost any stroke of the pen. They have rather allowed styles to develop themselves naturally, and are specially favourable to flowing curves, which are as easy as they are graceful in human penmanship.

Paper has for long been the common substance for miscellaneous purposes of ordinary writing, and has till recent times been formed solely from rags (chiefly of linen), reduced to a pulp, poured out on a frame in a thin watery sheet, and gradually dried and given consistence by the action of heat. It has been a popular belief, found in every book till 1886 (now entirely disproved, but probably destined to die hard), that the common yellowish thick paper, with rough fibrous edge, found especially in Greek MSS. till the fifteenth century, was paper of quite another sort, and made of cotton (*charta bombȳcǐna*, bombyx being usually silk, but also used of any fine fibre such as cotton). The microscope has at last conclusively shown that these two sorts are simply two different kinds of ordinary linen-rag paper.

A few facts about the dates at which papyrus, parchment and paper are found may be inserted here. The use of papyrus in Egypt is of great antiquity, and the earliest Greek and Latin MSS. we possess are on papyrus ; in the case of Greek of the fourth century B.C., in Latin of the first century A.D. It was freely exported to Greece and Rome, and, though it gradually gave way before parchment for the finest books, from the first century B.C. onwards, it was not till the tenth century A.D. that

in Egypt itself its use was abandoned. Practically
in about A.D. 935 its fabrication ceased, although for
Pontifical Bulls it was invariably used till A.D. 1022,
and occasionally till 1050. Parchment has also been
used from the earliest times; and its use was
revived, as we have seen, in the second century
before Christ, and lasted till the invention of
printing, after which it was reserved for sumptuous
editions, and for legal and other durable records.
Paper was first manufactured (outside China) at
Samarkand in Turkestan in about A.D. 750; and
even in Spain, where first it obtained a footing in
Europe (in the tenth century), it was imported from
the East, not being manufactured in the West till the
twelfth century; but from that time its use spread
rapidly. In England there was a paper-mill owned
by John Tate in 1495, when Bartholomæus Glanville's *De proprietatibus rerum* was issued on native
paper. Watermarks in paper (see p. 16) are entirely
a Western invention, found first towards the end of
the thirteenth century, and never found at all in
Oriental paper.

Besides stone, papyrus, parchment, and paper, the
materials used for writing, though numerous, are
rather curious than important. Tablets of wood,
hinged like a book and covered with wax, on which
letters were scratched with a small pointed metal rod
(*stilus*, whence our words *style*, *stiletto*, etc.), were
common at Rome in classical and later times, and
are believed to have suggested the form of our

ordinary books. For private accounts and notes
these wax tablets are said to have been in use in
Western Europe until the time of printing. Various
metals, especially lead, have been made use of to
bear writing ; and also bones (in prehistoric times),
clay inscribed when soft and then baked (as in
Assyria), potsherds (*ostraka*), leaves, and the like.

B.—*Forms of Books*

We now come to the forms of books—the way in
which they are made up. In the case of papyrus,
as has already been observed, we almost always find
the roll-form. The long strip was, of course, rolled
round a round rod or two rods (one at each end) when
not in use, much as a wall-map is at the present day.
With parchment the case has been different.
Though in classical times in Rome, so far as can
be judged, the roll-form was still in ordinary use
even when parchment was the material, and though,
in the form of court-rolls, pedigrees, and many legal
kinds of record, we are still familiar with the appearance of a roll, the tendency of writers on parchment
has been to prefer and perpetuate the form of
book best known at the present day, in which pages
are turned over by the reader, and no membranes
unrolled.

The normal formation of a parchment book in the
Middle Ages was this :—four pieces of parchment,
each roughly about 10 inches high and 18 inches
broad, were taken and were folded once across, so

that each piece formed four pages (two leaves) as
a basis for making a quarto volume. These pieces
were then fitted one inside another, so that the first
piece formed the 1st and 8th leaves, the second the
2nd and 7th, the third the 3rd and 6th, and the
fourth the two middle leaves of a complete section
of eight leaves or sixteen pages, termed technically
in Latin a *quaternio*, because made of four (*quatuor*)
pieces of parchment. When a sufficient number of
quaternions were thus formed to contain the pro-
jected book, they were sent in to the scribe for writing on, and were eventually bound. Many variations
of form, both smaller and larger than quarto, are
found, and often more or fewer pieces than four
make up the section or quire.

Paper was essentially different from parchment,
in that it could be made of larger size and folded
smaller; whereas the cost of skins was almost prohibitive, if very large and fine pieces were required.
As a fact, paper has almost always been used in book
and not roll-form. The normal formation of paper-
books has been this:— a piece about 12 inches high
by 16 inches wide was regarded as a standard size.
This was folded across along the dotted line *a b*, and

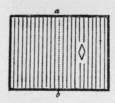

if this singly-folded sheet was re
garded as the basis of a section,
and the whole book was made up
of a set of these sections, it was
called a folio book; if, however,
the singly-folded sheet was folded

again across the dotted line *c d*, and *this* was treated as a section (containing four leaves or eight pages), the book made up of such sections was called a quarto. Once more, if the doubly-folded sheet was again folded along the dotted line *e f*, and this trebly-folded sheet was treated as a section (containing eight leaves or sixteen pages), the book was called an octavo. The methods of folding the sheet so as to produce a duodecimo, a 16mo, etc., and the use of half-sheets to form sections, are matters which concern printing rather than writing. But it should be clearly understood that, whereas we now mean by a folio a tall narrow book, by a quarto a shorter broad book, and by an octavo a short narrow book, judging by *size* and *shape ;* in the earlier days of paper, these terms indicated, *not* size or even shape, but form, that is to say, the way in which the sheets of paper were folded up to form sections ; and that it is only owing to the fact that a certain size of paper was generally adopted as a standard that the terms came to have their modern signification. So true is this, that some early folios are quite small, and many quartos larger or smaller than what we call quarto. But there is one infallible test of a true folio, quarto, or octavo. Observe the diamond on the figures on pp. 15-16, and the lines drawn across them. The diamond represents the *watermark*, a trade design (such as a jug, a unicorn, a pair of scissors, etc.)

inserted by the maker in every sheet, and the lines are ' chain-lines,' the marks where the wire frames supported the half liquid paper-sheet as it gathered consistency by being dried. The position of the watermark and the direction of the chain-lines were fortunately invariable, and therefore (as may be easily seen by a paper model) every true folio has the watermark in the centre of a page and the chain-lines perpendicular ; every quarto has the watermark in the centre of the back, not easy to see, and the lines horizontal ; and every octavo has a watermark at the top of the back at the inner edge, and the lines perpendicular. These points are *not* necessarily true of modern books.

C.—*Instruments and Ink*

On this subject few words are necessary. For hard substances and for wax and clay, a graving tool or pointed metal rod is necessary ; for papyrus and parchment and paper, a pen. Pens have till modern times always been of one of two kinds, either made of a reed (*calamus, arundo,* a reed-pen), or made of a quill, usually from a bird's feather (*penna,* a quill-pen). The latter appears to be the later in invention, but is found as early as the sixth century of our era.

Ink (*atramentum*) has hardly varied in composition from the earliest times, having been always formed in one of two ways : either, as was the common practice in classical times, by a mixture of soot with gum and water, which produces a black lustrous ink,

C

but is without much difficulty removed with a
sponge ; or by galls (gallic acid) with sulphate of
iron and gum, which is the modern method, though
also so ancient as to be found on the Herculanean
rolls. At Pompeii ink of this kind was found still
liquid after seventeen centuries of quiescence. The
chief coloured inks known to antiquity were red,
purple, green, and yellow : gold and silver liquids
were sometimes used, especially when the parchment had been stained purple to enhance the effect.
For the colours used in illumination, Chapter V. may
be consulted.

So far we have been concerned with passive substances prepared and presented to the scribe, to
become instinct with life when the message of the
author is consigned to the expectant page. Our
next chapters will naturally treat of the writing
itself, and of scribes and their ways, the living
elements in a book.

CHAPTER III

THE HISTORY OF WRITING

AFTER the invention of speech, the invention of writing was only a question of time. No race of human beings which could speak would rest for long contented with oral communication, but would endeavour, whether for the transmission of a message or for permanent record, to represent words by visible characters. And as early speech made large use of the imitative (onomatopœetic) faculty, so primitive writing made free use of pictures, first to represent material things, and then by a further advance of its infant powers to represent ideas suggested by those pictures. These two stages are known as *ideographic*, ideograms meaning either pictures or (for the second stage) pictorial symbols. It is curious to note that the contents of an ordinary printer's case of type show an ideogram still in use. What is ☞ but a 'pictorial symbol,' saying as clearly as in words, 'Look there!'? So, too, the 'Roman' numerals I, II, III, IIII are in all probability pictures of one, two, three, and four fingers held up, just as V is the whole hand, the four fingers being grouped together as one and the thumb as the other limb of the figure. X is probably

simply two Vs ; but the higher Roman numerals
were not needed by primitive man, and seem not to
be ideographic. Savages still use this picture-
language ; and Dr. Isaac Taylor, in his *History of
the Alphabet*, gives a striking illustration of a record
of a raid made by North American Indians in A.D.
1762, in which almost every part is pure picture
writing !

The third stage was perhaps the most momentous,
and consisted in fixing a written symbol, not to some
object or idea, but to a particular sound, whatever
objects or ideas that sound might call up ; as would
be the case if the mark   ☞   were not taken to
represent ' look ! ' or ' attend ! ' or ' there ! ' but
the *sound* ' there,' so that it would stand for ' there '
or (pretty nearly) ' their.' This, the ' phonographic '
stage, is the one in which we now are, and consists
naturally of three steps—(1) when the written
symbol represents a whole word, (2) when it expresses a single syllable, (3) when it represents a
single letter, as in our present alphabetical writing.
The first two of these may be illustrated by the use
of & for *et* in Latin, coupled with its usage in certain
centuries in any word containing -et-, so that we
find *fier&*, *perp&uus*, and the like ; for in these latter
examples the symbol means the sound *et* and not the
word *et*. The third is, of course, our own usage.

The letters which we use in writing and printing
have had a history which exhibits in most cases, in
spite of our imperfect records, every one of the five

stages described above. We will briefly trace this line, giving the ancestry of the English alphabet, and selecting the letters D and M for illustration.

The pedigree is this :—

		TILL	
Egyptian (Hieroglyphic),		—	} Hamitic.
Egyptian (Hieratic),		about 19th cent. B.C.	
Old Semitic,	.	—	} Semitic.
Phœnician,	.	about 1100 B.C.	
Old Greek,	.	close of 9th cent. B.C.	} Aryan.
Latin,	. .	about 600 A.D.	
English,	.	—	

The most extraordinary fact in this line is the transference of the alphabet on two separate occasions from one race of languages to another. Each race has its peculiar sounds, vowel and consonantal, and a transference of the symbols without the actual sounds would seem a hopeless and unworkable task. And our surprise is not lessened when we consider three points in which Semitic languages differ from all others—(1) nearly all are written from right to left, (2) the Semitic alphabet proper has no true vowels, (3) it has never varied from twenty-two letters, whereas the Aryan alphabets constantly vary in the number and phonetic value of the letters. For twenty-eight centuries have the Semitic languages preserved these peculiarities ; and that men were able to accomplish the feat of transference to and from a Semitic alphabet is a wonderful testimony to human powers of adaptation.

Among the earliest Egyptian Hieroglyphic writings preserved to us is that which is cut on a stone tablet [1] in the Ashmolean Museum at Oxford, and carries us back to a priest employed in the cult of the Egyptian king Send, not later than about 3000 B.C. This inscription is still one of the oldest known written records in the world. In this, as well as in later records, we find all five stages coexisting ! This fact will serve to impress on us the immense antiquity of Egyptian writing and of alphabetical writing, and the various rate at which civilization progresses ; for we find alphabetical symbols in B.C. 3000, and purely pictorial symbols in A.D. 1762, though the latter is as certainly prior in conception to the former as the dawn is before the day.

By the nineteenth century B.C. the ancient Hieroglyphic picture writing of Egypt was worn down to what is known as Hieratic, in which the symbols would not be at once recognized as pictures, though based on them. In about this century, probably just when the Israelites were in Egypt, the great transference took place : a Semitic people adopted the Egyptian symbols, using them for what is known as Old Semitic, as seen in the Siloam inscription at Jerusalem, and the Moabite Stone now (so far as it has survived) in the Louvre at Paris.

We have no evidence whatever of the way in which the Phœnicians acquired and adopted the Old Semitic symbols ; and till recently the weak link of

[1] See illustration opposite p. 106.

the whole chain of connexion was at this point,
the doubt being, not whether the earliest Greek
writing was deduced from Phœnician (for that has
been universally conceded), but whether and how
Phœnician came from Old Semitic. However, the
opinions of De Rougé and others, as described, for
instance, in Isaac Taylor's *History of the Alphabet*,
have till lately been generally accepted, and even
now no constructive theory has been advanced to
take their place. The general effect of the discoveries of Sir Arthur Evans and others is to show
that the history of the alphabet is more complex
than was at one time thought. De Rougé's theory
has no doubt been rudely shaken, and it has been
shown that all kinds of direct transmission have
taken place, as from Egypt and from Philistia to
Crete. *Non nostrum tantas——*, but it may still
well be true that much of the alphabet passed along
De Rougé's lines of transference.

It is instructive to see what solid truth is thus to
be found in the old Greek legend of Cadmus, which
represents him as a Phœnician of Tyre, yet intimately connected with Egypt, and as having
introduced into Greece from Phœnicia or Egypt an
alphabet of sixteen letters. For the Greeks did most
undoubtedly derive their own alphabet from the
Phœnician, adapting Semitic symbols to an Aryan
set of sounds; and caused it to be used in Greece
itself and over all the shores of the Ægean. The
Greek alphabet thus acquired was carried by the

Chalcidians of Eubœa, at about the end of the
ninth century B.C., to one of their Italian colonies,
the well-known town of Cumæ in Campania, and,
for some reason not recorded in history, was taken
up by the one Italian people destined to found an
empire, the earliest inhabitants of Rome. The
result may be told in Dr. Isaac Taylor's words : ' It
became the alphabet of Latin Christendom, and the
literary alphabet of Europe and America. It is
now, with the single exception of the Arabic, the only
alphabet possessing any claim to cosmopolitan
extension.'

The letter D is a good example of the changes
above described :—In Hieroglyphic, it is a view of
the hand, the thumb projecting above (see plate
opposite p. 106, in the cartouche). Clearly the essential point about the figure is, not the view of the
fingers, but the projection of the thumb ; accordingly in Hieratic the form is ⌐⌐, preserving
the thumb-line. In Old Semitic this became △,
an angular form due to inscriptions (see p. 6),
perpetuated in the Greek Δ, but rounded in Latin
to D, and in later forms to ꝺ, d, d.

Or take the letter M. In Hieroglyphic this is a
side view of an owl, with its face turned towards
the spectator,   . The owl was *mulak*, and so
when the symbol became syllabic it represented
mu, and when alphabetic *m*. Later the owl loses

its ears and tail, but still recalls the picture,   𓄿 ;

in Hieratic it has come to   𝟯, the upper curve representing the head and the lower the rounded back, all else being dropped as unessential. This in Old Semitic appears as   𝑀, in Greek as M, in Latin capitals the same, and in smaller letters, from an attempt to write it quickly, *m*.

Let us now trace in rather more detail the history of writing in Western Europe from Roman times to our own. Much of the significance and most of our appreciation of the manuscript volumes to be hereafter described will be lost if we do not see clearly, even if in outline only, the changes of writing which mark the principal eras and nationalities which succeeded the empire of Rome. The table on page 26 will illustrate the course and connexion of each kind.

The great fundamental division of writing, which is applicable to all periods and peoples, is that which puts on one side the common, ordinary hand in private use,—the hand which we and all our ancestors have used in writing letters, setting down accounts, keeping diaries, and scribbling,—which is Cursive ; and puts on the other side the writing reserved for literary monuments, the ornamental, set, careful, impressive hand which we now, owing to the printing-press, hardly know, but in which monks wrote out chronicles, in which old service books were produced, in which legal and regal transactions, and everything which seemed to deserve

HANDWRITINGS OF WESTERN EUROPE.

("iv." = 4th. cent. A.D., *i.e.* 301-400 A.D.: and so with the rest).

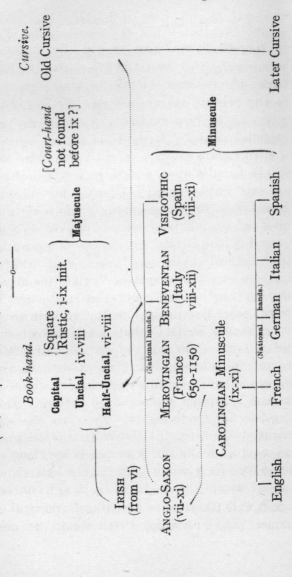

Cursive.
Old Cursive

Later Cursive

Book-hand.

Capital { Square
        { Rustic, i-ix init.
Uncial, iv-viii

Majuscule

[*Court-hand* not found before ix?]

Half-Uncial, vi-viii

IRISH (from vi)

ANGLO-SAXON (vii-xi)

(National hands.)

MEROVINGIAN (France 650-1150)

BENEVENTAN (Italy viii-xii)

VISIGOTHIC (Spain viii-xi)

Minuscule

CAROLINGIAN MINUSCULE (ix-xi)

(National | hands.)

English   French   German   Italian   Spanish

immortal record, were enshrined. We ourselves
usually have two hands, if we only notice them, a
careless private one, and a formal calligraphic style.
⁀Our survey of Western handwritings naturally
begins with the Roman Capital writing. The sudden
remark of every one who is shown a specimen for the
first time is, how extremely like our own printed
capitals! Take a facsimile of a MS. written in
Roman square capitals—every letter from A to Z
will be found shaped as ours, except W, which does
not exist in Latin, and J, U, which are not distinct
from I, V. How this comes to be, in a subject where
all is change, will be seen as we proceed.

Pure square *Capitals* are hard to find in writing as
distinguished from inscriptions, but exist, for
instance, in the fragments of Virgil in the library of
St. Gall (fourth or fifth century A.D. : *Palæogr. Soc.* i.
plate 208). But the first declension from the pure
type, namely Rustic Capitals, is not uncommon. In
this all the letters are capital, but are thinner,
compressed laterally as it were, while the numerous
horizontal strokes on the right hand of an ordinary
capital are often prolonged to the left. Thus E
becomes E, T becomes I. The first great
change is, however, the *Uncial* hand, which perhaps
meaning originally letters an inch (*uncia*) long, came
to be used for a kind in which all the letters are still
capital, except that A, D, E, H, M, Q have become
ᴀ, ᴆ, ᴄ, ʜ, ᴍ, ꞯ. The next step is the still com-
moner *Half-Uncial* hand, in which the general

appearance is no longer capital, and indeed only N
and F are clearly and unmistakably of that nature ;
the rest approximating in shape rather to our small
printed letters, as in p, m, ſ (s), 𝒓 (r). It will be
understood that the references in this chapter are to
the ordinary, natural hand of a scribe, not to the
artificial and ornamental hands reserved for titles
and incipits or colophons. It is due to the latter
that the plate opposite p. 31 is able to present us
with four styles in one example.

In the seventh and eighth centuries we find the
first tendency to form national hands, resulting in
the Merovingian or Frankish hand, the Beneventan
of Italy, and the Visigothic of Spain. These are the
first difficult hands, except Old Cursive ; and when
we remember that the object of writing is to be clear
and distinct, and that the test of a good style is that
it seizes on the essential points in which letters differ,
and puts aside the flourishes and ornaments which
disguise the simple form, we shall see how much a
strong influence was needed to prevent writing from
being ruined by the national hands. That influence
was found in Charles the Great.

In the field of writing it has been granted to no
person but Charles the Great to influence profoundly
the history of the alphabet. With rare insight and
rarer taste he discountenanced the prevalent Merovingian hand, and substituted an eclectic hand,
known as the Carolingian Minuscule, which may still
be regarded as a model of clearness and elegance.

The chief instrument in this reform was Alcuin of
York, whom Charles placed, partly for this purpose,
at the head of the School of Tours in A.D. 796. The
selection of an Englishman for the post naturally
leads us to inquire what hands were then used in
England, and what amount of English influence the
Carolingian Minuscule, the foundation of our modern
styles, exhibits. But we must begin with Ireland.

If we gaze in wonder on the personal influence of
Charles the Great in reforming handwriting, we shall
be still more struck by the spectacle presented to us
by Ireland in the sixth, seventh, and eighth centuries.
It is the great marvel in the history of palæography.
Modern historians have at last appreciated the blaze
of life, religious, literary, and artistic, which was
kindled in the ' Isle of Saints ' within a century after
St. Patrick's coming (which was about A.D. 450) ;
how the enthusiasm kindled by Christianity in the
Celtic nature so far transcended the limits of the
island, and indeed of Great Britain, that Irish
missionaries and monks were soon found in the chief
religious centres of Gaul, Germany, Switzerland, and
North Italy, while foreigners found their toilsome
way to Ireland to learn Greek. But less prominence
has been given to the artistic side of this great reflex
movement from West to East than to the other two.
The simple facts attest that in the seventh century,
when our earliest existing Irish MSS. were written,
we find not only a style of writing (or indeed two)
distinctive, national, and of a high type of excellence,

but also a school of illumination which, in the
combined lines of mechanical accuracy and intricacy,
in fertile invention of form and figure and of striking
arrangements of colour, has never been surpassed.
And this is in the seventh century—the nadir of the
rest of Europe.

The great Irish school of writing and painting
passed over to England by way of the monasteries
founded by Irish monks in Scotland. There St.
Columba (*d.* 597) founded the first Scottish monastery at Iona, and thence the first monastery in
England was founded by St. Aidan at Lindisfarne
or Holy Island, off the Northumbrian coast (A.D.
635). But in 597 St. Augustine of Canterbury had
landed in Kent, and with him brought the old
Roman half-uncial hand still to be seen (among
other volumes) in the two Latin books of the
Gospels, traditionally supposed to be among those
actually brought by Augustine, and now preserved
at Cambridge and Oxford. These two forces, the
Roman and the Irish half-uncial hands, may be said
to have met at the Council of Whitby in 664. Was
Augustine or Aidan, Rome or Ireland, destined to
supply us with our English national hand? The
Irish hand won the day, and the ' Hiberno-Saxon '
(or ' Insular ') hand became the national hand of
England, Scotland, and Ireland, until the Norman
Conquest at last reversed the national victory of
Whitby, and the Roman or Continental hand, which
had never wholly lost its footing in England,

ſcōrum· per dñm nrm Jii· kt· oct· idest xx·
viiii· die m· ſept· dedic· baſilice· ſci· angeli· mich

SQVIMIRO
RDINEANGELORu
miſteria hominumq; diſpenſaſ·
concede· propiciaſ ut quibuſ abi
miniſtrantibuſ in cuclo ſemper
adſiſtitur ab hiſ in terra utcanta
muniuur· per dñm.   SECRETA·
Hoſtaſabi dñe ludiſ offerimuſ ſupplicater de

PLATE III : SACRAMENTARY (9th cent., Continental). Exhibiting Square Capital, here coloured [l. 3], Rustic Capital [ll. 1, 2, 9], Uncial [l. 4], and Carolingian Minuscule.

excluded its rival. It is certain, then, that Alcuin
was trained in Insular calligraphy, so that we may
be surprised to find that the writing which, under
Charles the Great, he developed at Tours, bears
hardly a trace of the style to which he was accustomed. *En revanche*, in the ornamentation and
illumination of the great Carolingian volumes which
have come down to our times, we find those per-
sistent traces of English and Irish work which we
seek for in vain in the plainer Carolingian writing.

This minuscule superseded all others almost
throughout the empire of Charles the Great, and
during the ninth, tenth, and eleventh centuries
underwent comparatively little modification. Even
in the two next centuries, though it is subject to
general modification, national differences are hardly
observable, and we need only distinguish two large
divisions, the group of Northern Europe (England,
North France, and the Netherlands), and the
Southern (South France, Italy, and Spain). The
two exceptions are, that Germany, both in writing
and painting, has always stood apart, and has lagged
behind the other nations of Western Europe in its
development ; and that England retained her Hiberno-Saxon or Insular hand till the great Conquest
of 1066. It may be said that the twelfth century
produced the finest writing ever known—a large, free
and flowing form of the minuscule of Tours. In the
next century comes in the angular Gothic hand, the
difference between which and the twelfth century

hand may be fairly understood by a comparison
of ordinary German and Roman type. In the
thirteenth, fourteenth, and fifteenth centuries the
writing of each country may be discerned, while the
general tendency is towards complication, use of
abbreviations and contractions, and development of
unessential parasitic forms of letters (see plates
facing pp. 1, 64, 66). The study of these styles is
a study of details, and as such needs the manuals
mentioned in the Bibliographies in App. C.

How then, to revert to a previous question, does
it come about that our modern capitals are like those
of ancient Rome, and our ordinary letters, as
printed, so like the Carolingian minuscule? This
we can now answer. The early printers of the
second half of the fifteenth century took as their
models one or other of two kinds of letters, either the
current Gothic hand, of which modern German type
is the direct outcome, or the luxurious style which—
itself a revival of the clear twelfth century writing
—was adopted in Italy by the scribes of the
Renaissance. This latter set of forms, through the
collective good sense of successive generations, won
its way, and secured for all future time the neat,
easily read and sensible forms of the familiar Roman
type. We see, then, that readers of the present day
owe their eyesight and their comfort to (1) the
revival of pure forms of an old Roman kind by
Charles the Great ; (2) the almost accidental fact
that the later Carolingian writing of the twelfth

century was imitated by the Italian scribes of the fifteenth ; (3) the happy natural selection by which printers chose this revived kind of letter. Had any one of these links failed, our type would probably have failed to attain its undoubted excellence.

Of court-hand—the stiff, formal writing affected by law courts and royal chanceries—our space does not allow us to treat. It began to diverge from the literary hand in the ninth century, and after the twelfth becomes more and more artificial and perplexing till at least the seventeenth. It is allowable to doubt whether this is wholly unintentional, and to suggest that in essence court-hand has been more or less an instrument which has helped the lawyers of past times to make their profession exclusive, secret, and mysterious in the eyes of the laity.

Abbreviation and Contraction

A student, when he has mastered the difficulties connected with the forms of letters—which indeed can almost be met in the case of any particular MS. by a skilful use of methods used in solving cryptograms,—will find himself face to face with the serious trouble of abbreviations and contractions, especially in MSS. later than the ninth century. He finds *mia* written for *miseria* or for *misericordia*, he finds *mundus* written *mūd'* and the like. Till Ludwig Traube (*d.* 1907) arose, these difficulties could only be overcome by empiric rules and facts, but that great palæographer (who occupied a place

D

among palæographers almost as eminent as that of Henry Bradshaw among bibliographers) discovered principles where others only saw sequences of fact.

Traube was the first who distinguished the true relation between the two great systems of Abbreviation (by which term is implied any way of writing a word in short form, although in practice Shorthand is excluded from its scope as being too artificial and mechanical), namely Abbreviation by Suspension and Abbreviation by Contraction. The former class consists of a shortening by suspending the pen, simply not writing the whole of the word (as in A.D. for Anno Domini, Nom̄ for Nomen). The latter is a shortening by giving the beginning and end of the word, and often an important letter in the middle, and recognizing certain definite symbols akin to Shorthand (as in the examples given on p. 33).

The history of these two methods is interesting. The earliest of the two at Rome was Suspension, which starts the word for you but gives no inkling of the termination. Examples are H.S.E. (*Hic situs est*), on sepulchral monuments, S.V.B.E. (*Si vales bene est*), in letters. But it was especially taken up by lawyers who used numerous forms like .Tm. for *Testamentum* (where the *m* is the first *m*, not the termination [1]). This system, though subject to

---

[1] It was allowable in Suspension to give the *first* letter of a syllable in the middle of a word, as well as the first letter of the whole word, but never the termination. Thus *noster* could be .N. or .NT.

the fortunate limitation that the suspended word must be in common use, and therefore partly self-suggestive to educated men, developed so many ambiguities that in the fourth century of our era it began to give way before the insidious approach of a rival system.

The system of Contraction started with the Jews, who were accustomed to omit the vowels in the sacred name of Jahwe or Jehovah. It was transferred by Hellenizing Jews to Greek scribes through Greek translations of the Hebrew Scriptures. From the Greeks it passed to Rome. One of the proofs of Jewish origin is that the usage, even in Latin, was at first absolutely confined to just five Sacred Names:—

Deus (*ds*), Jesus (*ihs*), Christus (*xps*), Spiritus (*sps*), and Dominus (*dns*). The Greek stage is obvious from the *h* of *ihs* and the *x p* of *xps*. This limited set of contractions is found in Rome from about A.D. 300, but in Africa and Gaul from about A.D. 410, and in Spain before A.D. 450.

But the floodgates soon opened wider, and other ecclesiastical terms suffered contraction, and by the sixth century lay terms were admitted, and the vogue of Suspension was over. A remarkable example of the fight between the Old and the New is

afforded by the seemingly insignificant word *noster*,
which derived its importance at first from the
common ending of a liturgical prayer, ' per Dominum
nostrum Iesum Christum', and the like. The oldest
form of abbreviation was .N. (Suspension), but
its ambiguity was its ruin. The new system
quickly killed it, substituting the type *ñ̄* (if
we take the genitive case *nostri* as a convenient
case for describing types). But even this was
ambiguous (*n̄o* = *nostro*, colliding with *non*,
and *ñ̄a* with *nam*, etc.). So a rival *n̄r̄i*
type arose, which waged a curious and definite war
with the older *ñ̄* type. Thus in Italy and
France the war raged from about A.D. 700 to 900 :
in Ireland and England only from 700 to 800 : in
Germany from 800 to nearly 1000. In all these
battlefields the *n̄r̄i* type won, and throughout
the Middle Ages *noster* is *n̄r̄* , *nostri* *n̄r̄i* ,
nostro *n̄r̄o*, *nostrum* *n̄r̄m* , etc. This example
is a specimen of the fighting which went on everywhere, and as the campaigns are pretty well known,
we obtain a valuable instrument for dating old
MSS.

However, for MSS. which my readers are
likely to come across, it may be assumed that the
full system of Abbreviation by Contraction is in
force, and a few details of its chief forms may be
given.

Abbreviation by Contraction

This was of three chief kinds in the Middle Ages :—
(A). Abbreviation by abbreviative *signs*, seven in number :—

	Form.	*Position.*	*Value.*
i.	— or ~	above preceding letter	*m* or *n*.
ii.	ς or S	ditto	*er, re, ri, ir* or *r*.
iii.	η	above, but after, preceding letter	*us*.
iv.	2 or $\}$	above preceding letter	*ur*.
v.	$\mathfrak{I}$	on line	*con*, or *com*.
vi.	:, then ;, then $\mathfrak{Z}$	on line	(*q*)*ue, et, -*(*b*)*us*, or *m*.
vii.	4	on line	*-rum*.

Thus *mūd$\mathfrak{I}$* (i, iii), *$\mathfrak{I}$ctat²* (v, ii, iv), *plurıb;* (vi), *mensa4* (vii).

There are also a few general signs, such as :—

Exōn (= Exonia, Exonienses, etc.) *re$\varrho\varphi$*

(= regis), $\wp$ = ser-). P has a peculiar set :

$\bar{p}$ = pre, $\wp$ = *per*, $\wp$ = pro.

(B). Abbreviation by *position* of letters.
i. Vowels over preceding letters indicate suppression of *r* before or after the vowel.

Thus *$\acute{e}$men* = *crimen*, *$\acute{u}bi$* = *uerbi*, not *ubi*.

ii. Q omits its u, if the vowel following is written over the q. Thus $\overset{o}{q}$ = *quo*.

(C). Abbreviation by *omission.*

i. The first and last letters must be given, and usually one medial; the word must be in common use; and as in all cases of Contraction, a line must be drawn over the contracted part, e.g. $\overline{s\hspace{-1mm}f\hspace{-1mm}r}$ (*similiter*), $\overline{vi;}$ (*videlicet*, our *viz.*), $\overline{lre}$ (*litere*), $\overline{oro}$ (*oratio*).

ii. The following are typical, but cannot all be reduced to the foregoing principles :—

$\overline{ao}$ (-*atio*)	$\overline{qm}$ (*quoniam*) ⎫		
$\overline{bti}$ (*beati*)	$\overline{qn}$ (*quando*) ⎬		
$\overline{dci}$ (*dicti*)	$\overline{tm}$ (*tantum*) ⎫		
$\overline{fr}$ (*frater* : so $\overline{mr}$,	$\overline{tn}$ (*tamen*) ⎭		
$\overline{pr}$)	∿ (*est*),	*l* (*id est*),	
	n (*enim*),	7 (*et*),	
$\overline{nr}$ (*noster* : so $\overline{ur}$, *uester*)	(*igitur*),	(*ergo*)	

It is happily true of Latin, though not of Greek, that contractions are seldom in any way ambiguous, though a want of familiarity and of special knowledge may make them seem formidable to a beginner.

Such, in briefest outline, has been the history of the handwritings which most nearly concern us. Enough has been said, it may be hoped, to enable our readers to fit roughly into their places the volumes which we may have to describe in future chapters as of such and such an age, style, or nationality. The plates in this volume will supply some further help, and reference may be made especially to the *Introduction to Greek and Roman Palæography* by Sir E. Maunde Thompson (2nd ed., Oxford, 1912).

CHAPTER IV

SCRIBES AND THEIR WAYS

In Greece and Rome, scribes (γραμματεις, *grammateis*; καλλιγράφοι, *calligraphoi*; *librarii, scribæ*) formed a distinct and important profession. We have, however, very little direct evidence which would enable us to characterize in any special way their modes of work. We know that in Rome the work was done both quickly and cheaply; the poet Martial, for instance, reminds a friend (*Epigr.* i. 117) that for five denarii (about 3s. 6d.) he could buy the whole of his first book of *Epigrams.* It would seem natural that when many copies of such a work as Martial's *Epigrams* or Virgil's *Æneid* were needed, dictation should be resorted to, and we can picture a room with twenty or more scribes writing from the dictation of some clear-voiced reader; but the evidence of dictation is so scanty, that we are driven to conclude that scribes almost invariably copied from a volume in front of them in silence, as was certainly the case in the scriptoria of monasteries. Alcuin, who describes the copying work at York, seems to know nothing of it, and the word *dictare,* used in connexion with writing, means 'to compose,'

not dictate.[1] The only dictation which was common
was when a letter or message was dictated by its
composer to swift-penned *notarii*.

But when we reach the age of monasticism, we find
full details of the interior and working of the writing-
room or scriptorium of a normal religious establish-
ment. Though it is true that the great Benedictine
Order, and its daughter the Cistercian, distinctly
encouraged the study of literature, even other than
theological, and that, as a fact, more than half the
literary work of Europe was done within the walls
of religious houses, yet it will be found on examination that the important centres of writing and
illumination were not numerous, such as, in England,
Canterbury, Winchester, St. Alban's, Durham, and
Glastonbury ; while, if we regard the smaller
houses, since literature and study were after all only a
secondary feature in the theory of monastic life,
only a small proportion of monks were allowed to take
up the work, and often, we may be sure, by accident
or design, the copying would fall into second-rate
hands, and, not being in especial repute, be neglected
or ill done. Few even of the largest abbeys rose to
such full appreciation of the claims of literature,
whether reading, composing, or copying, as to have
a *historiographus*, or official recorder of the general

---

[1] Thus—

    ' Hic Augustini liber est simul atque Frowini :
    Alter dictavit, alter scribendo notavit,'

only states that Frowinus was the scribe, and that he had copied
a treatise of St. Augustine ; see also p. 148.

and local history of the time (such as was Matthew
Paris from 1236 to 1259, at St. Alban's), who would
give lustre and importance to the whole writing
department of the house.

Yet at certain times and places the scribe was
held in quite conspicuous honour. In Ireland, for
instance, in the seventh and eighth centuries, the
penalty for shedding his blood was as great as that
for killing a bishop or abbot ; and in Scotland,
' scriba ' was regarded as an honourable addition to
a bishop's name. Adamnan's *Life of St. Columba*
is full of allusions to the art of writing, in which the
Saint himself excelled ; and it is owing to its
prominence that such stories are permanently
recorded, as of the men who dropped a MS. into
a vessel of water, and upset the Saint's own inkhorn.
And the vivid picture given us by Sir T. D. Hardy
in the Preface to the third volume of the *Materials
relating to the History of Great Britain*, of the estab-
lishment at St. Alban's, shows a favourable aspect
of the life of copyists in the largest houses.

The scriptorium of an ordinary Benedictine monastery was a large room, usually over the chapter-
house. When no special room was devoted to the
purpose, separate little studies were often made in
the cloisters, each scribe having a window to himself,
as may still be seen in the exquisite cloisters of
Gloucester Cathedral (once St. Peter's Abbey) ; but
these carrels were fully open on one side to the
cloister walk, and it was quite exceptional for a

copyist to be allowed a cell or room in any way
private. The whole room, or set of studies, was
under the general discipline of the monastery, but
had special superadded rules of its own. These
rules, as preserved to us in certain Benedictine
statutes, are as stringent as can well be imagined.
Artificial light was entirely forbidden for fear of
injuring the manuscripts ; and to prevent idleness
and interruption, no one was allowed to enter the
room besides the scribes, except certain of the higher
officers of the abbey. The *Armarius* was the
special officer who had charge of the scriptorium ;
but even he had no power to give out work to be
done without the abbot's leave. He had to provide
all that was necessary for the work—desks, ink,
parchment, pens, pen-knives, pumice-stone for
smoothing the surface of the parchment, awls to
give guiding marks for ruling lines, reading frames
to hold the books to be copied, rulers and weights to
keep down the pages. The scribe himself was forbidden to make any alteration in the text, even when
the original which he was copying was obviously
wrong. Absolute silence was enjoined ; and as,
nevertheless, some method of communication was
necessary, there was a great variety of signs in use.
If a scribe needed a book, he extended his hands and
made a movement as of turning over leaves. If it
was a missal that was wanted, he superadded the
sign of a cross ; if a psalter, he placed his hands on
his head in the shape of a crown (a reference to King

David) ; if a lectionary, he pretended to wipe away
the grease (which might easily have fallen upon it
from a candle) ; if a small work was needed, not a
Bible or service book, but some inferior tractate, he
placed one hand on his stomach and the other before
his mouth.   Finally, if a pagan work was required,
he first gave the general sign, and then scratched
his ear in the manner of a dog !

Besides the monks who acted as scribes and
illuminators, there were three classes of secular
scribes, who would only come to the monastery when
their services were needed—*illuminatores*, when the
abbey could not itself provide men capable of
finishing off the manuscript by rubrication and
painting ; *librarii*, a common kind of hack scribe ;
and *notarii*, who would be required for legal purposes, such as drawing up a deed or will.

It is not to be wondered at that the customs of a
particular monastery, or group of monasteries,
should result in a particular localized style of
writing.   The study of these local peculiarities has
not yet been carried far, but will no doubt be a
fruitful source of information in the future.   For
example, it was at one time the custom to ascribe to
the hand of Matthew Paris all volumes written in a
peculiar thirteenth century style, with the long stems
of certain letters broken-backed or bent, and distinguished by peculiar orthography, such as *imfra*
for *infra*.   It was discovered by Sir T. Duffus Hardy
that this writing was from the school of writing

PLATE IV : SCRIPTORIUM (1455. French).

prevalent at St. Alban's at that time, and not invariably the autograph of the historiographer
himself. Many forms of letters were absolutely
peculiar to a place, such as the M of St. Mary's
Abbey at York and the Q of the Austin Canons of
Carlisle.

Let us now consider how a scribe would act at the
beginning of his six-hour [1] daily task. A section of
plain parchment is brought to him to be written on,
each sheet still separate from the others, though
loosely put in the order and form in which it will
be subsequently bound. First, when the style and
general size of the intended writing have been fixed,
which would be a matter of custom, the largest style
being reserved for psalters and other books to be
used for public services on a desk or lectern, the
sheets have to be ruled. Down each side of the
page, holes were pricked at proper intervals with an
awl, or metal wheel bearing spikes on its circum-
ference, and a hard, dry, metal stilus was used to
draw the lines from hole to hole, with others perpendicular to mark off the margins ; space was also
left for illuminations if it could be estimated before-
hand. The stilus made a furrow on one side of the
parchment and raised a ridge on the other side, and
was carried right across a whole sheet of parchment.
This ruling was not such a simple matter as it might

[1] ' Ardua scriptorum præ cunctis artibus ars est :
Difficilis labor est, durus quoque flectere colla,
Et membranas *bis ternas* sulcare per horas.'
                    (*Anon.*, 9th cent. ?)

seem, and deserves further detail, because the regularity of the system by which it was done enables us to settle some curious points where a manuscript is imperfect. First, it must be noted that the two sides of a piece of parchment are seldom alike ; one is usually smoother and whiter (the original flesh-side), and the other rougher and yellowish (the hair-side). Now a quaternion (see p. 15) was almost always so arranged that wherever the book was opened, the two pages presented to the eye were *both* hair-side or *both* flesh-side. Sir E. Maunde Thompson lays down as a general rule that in Greek MSS. the first page of a section generally exhibited a flesh-side, and in Latin MSS. a hair-side. Secondly,—although the point has not been fully investigated,—at any rate in Greek MSS. of the ninth, tenth and eleventh centuries, the first page of a quaternion usually exhibited a set of *ridges*, and consequently the second page a set of furrows, when ruled. Putting what has been said together (it can readily be understood from a paper model), the normal arrangement of a Greek quaternion would be—   and for Latin—

Page.	Side.	Ruling.	Page.	Side.	Ruling.
1	flesh	ridges	1	hair	ridges
2-3	hair	furrows	2-3	flesh	furrows
4-5	flesh	ridges	4-5	hair	ridges
6-7	hair	furrows,	6-7	flesh	furrows
etc., until			etc., until		
16	flesh	ridges	16	hair	ridges.

Now, observe the use of these dull facts by an example. The celebrated Greek 'Codex Venetus' of the *Iliad* of Homer has at the beginning five leaves of introductory matter of a peculiarly interesting kind, being a unique account of Homer, and an abstract (not complete) of the poems composing the Epic Cycle. It is clear from the rest of the volume, which is made up of regular quaternions, that these five leaves are the relics of an original eight forming a quaternion. The question which has agitated scholars is the exact order in which these five leaves should be arranged. In 1881 the MS. was investigated to see if the principles of the normal arrangement of leaves with respect to hair and flesh sides, and with respect to furrows and ridges, would make impossible any of the five theories of arrangement. It was found that three of the five could be put 'out of court' at once by these considerations, leaving the important question reduced to the comparative claims of two only —a result well worth the investigation. Doubtless some puzzling questions of perturbed order in other manuscripts will in time yield to the application of similar principles.

The scribe has now his ruled leaves before him, his pen and ink in readiness, and the volume to be copied on a desk beside him : he may begin to transcribe. How simple this seems ! He is forbidden to correct, but must simply copy down letter for letter what is before him ; no responsibility, except for power of reading and for accuracy, is laid on him.

Yet all who know human nature, or who have studied palæography, will acknowledge that the probability against two consecutive leaves being really correctly transcribed is about a hundred to one. The causes of ' transcriptional error ' will be treated in Chap. VI. ; so that here it need only be said that the wonder is not that there is so much cause for critical treatment of the text of an ancient author, but that there is so little. When the copyist had finished a quaternion, the writing was often compared with the original by another person (διορθωτής, *diorthōtes* ; in Latin, corrector). Next, the sheets of a completed work were given over to the rubricator, who inserted in red or other colour titles, sometimes concluding notes (called colophons), liturgical directions, lists of chapters, headlines, and the like ; and finally, if need were, to the illuminator. Nothing then remained, but that the binder's art should sew together the sections, and put them in their covering ; a few words on which may here, for completeness' sake, be added, although the subject is fully treated in another volume in this series.

The common binding in the Middle Ages for books of some size and interest was leather, plain or ornamented, white or brown, fastened over solid wooden boards, with raised bands, four or five or more in number, across the back. The sewing of the sheets and passing of the thread over these bands usually results in a firmness and permanence which no ordinary modern book possesses : not infrequently the solid oak sides may have given way under violent treatment from too great rigidity, while the sewing remains perfectly sound. In general, however, the oak sides are as permanent as the back, and the solid pegging, by which the parchment strings issuing from the thread-sewn back are wedged into the small square holes and grooves cut in the inner oak sides, is a sight worth seeing for workmanship and indestructibility. But for appearance' sake in early mediæval times the finest books received an ivory, silver, or even gold binding, and the sides were carved or worked into embossed figures and set with jewels ; and sometimes even wooden sides were highly ornamented. Thus the Latin Gospel of St. John, taken from the tomb of St. Cuthbert, and now at Stonyhurst, is described as bound (in the tenth or eleventh century) in boards of thin wood covered with red leather, the obverse cover containing in the centre a raised ornament of Celtic design, and above and below small panels, with interlaced work graven on them and coloured. Of the finer kind, a Latin Psalter in the British Museum, written for Melissenda, Countess of Anjou, in the twelfth century, is an example, in which the sides are of carved ivory and set with turquoises. Perhaps the finest collection of these jewelled bindings in England is in the John Rylands Library at Manchester. In Ireland—but rarely elsewhere—we find a *theca* or ' cumdach,' a case in which a volume was kept ; and on this, instead of

E

the volume itself, the richest work was lavished. A
few still remain, as those of the Stowe Missal and of
St. Columba's Psalter, both of the eleventh century ;
but the rapacity of rough times has left few of the
grander bindings intact.   It is pleasant to read that
in the twelfth century England was before all foreign
nations in binding,—London, Winchester, and Durham having distinctive styles, known from the
designs stamped or traced on the leather sides, which
in all cases consist in the main of a parallelogram
formed by small dies, filled up by circles and portions
of circles in great variety. But the history of
binding belongs to the subject of printed books
rather than to that of manuscripts, for the great
majority of bindings now valued are subsequent to
the invention of printing.

The cost of writing, illumination, and binding is an
interesting subject, and though ample material for
settling the question exists, not much has as yet
been brought together.

In classical times, as we have seen (p. 40), a copy
of the 1st book of Martial's *Epigrams* (about 850
Latin lines of verse) cost only about 3s. 6d. in Rome :
and probably the competition of skilled scribes kept
the price down to a level comparable with printed
books at the present day.   In the monasteries of the
Middle Ages we naturally find no mention of cost of
writing, as the monk's work was part of his ordinary
duty, but the cost of materials and the time taken
are not infrequently recorded.   In the case of

professional scribes employed at monasteries, there
is, of course, mention of remuneration, as at Ely in
1372, where one received 43s. 4d. with a tunic as for
a year's work ; and the pay of a common scribe in
1300 was ½d. a day, equal to about 7½d. of our
money, while five dozen skins of parchment cost
only 2s. 6d.

A few examples of cost of production may be
given in chronological order.

About A.D. 1380, as Professor Middleton shows,
John Prust, Canon of Windsor, received 75s. 8d. for
writing and illuminating a *Textus Evangelii* (*i.e.* a
book of the liturgical Gospels, an Evangeliarium),
some of the items being,

	s.	d.
19 quaterni of parchment at /8, . . .	12	8
Ink, ...	1	2
Vermilion, ...		9
Commons (the writer's meat and drink) for 18		
weeks at /10, ...	15	0
Stipend, ...	13	4
Illumination, ...	4	3
Binding, ...	3	4

In 1453, John Reynbold agreed at Oxford to write
out the last three books of Duns Scotus's Commentary on the Sentences of Peter Lombard, in quarto,
for 2s. 2d. each book.   A transcript in folio by this
Reynbold of part of this work on the Sentences is in
both Merton and Balliol College Libraries at Oxford,
one dated 1451.

In 1467 the *Paston Letters* show that a writer and illuminator at Bury St. Edmund's received for producing a Psalter or other liturgical book, adding musical notes, illuminating, and binding, 100s. 2d.

For viij hole vynets (*i.e.* vignettes, small miniatures)
. . . prise the vynett xij*d*, ...   viij*s*
Item for xxj demi-vynets . . . prise the demi-
vynett, iiij*d*, ...   vij*s*
Item for Psalmes letters xv^c (1500) and di' (a half,
1550 in all) . . . the prise of c, iiij*d*,   .   .   v*s* ij*d*
Item for p'ms (primers ?) letters lxiij^c . . . prise of
c, j*d*, ...   v*s* iij*d*
Item for wrytynge of a quare and demi . . . prise
the quayr xx*d*, ...   ij*s* vj*d*
Item for wrytenge of a calender, ...   xij*d*
Item for iij quayres of velym, prise the quayr xx*d*,   v*s*
Item for notynge (musical notation) of v quayres
and ij leves, prise of the quayr viij*d*,   .   .   iij*s* vij*d*
Item for capital drawynge iij^c and di', the prise,   .   iij*d*
Item for floryshynge of capytallis, v^c,   .   .   .   v*d*
Item for byndynge of the boke,   .   .   .   xij*s*
                                            c*s* ij*d*

In 1468-71 a scribe received for a Lectionary, a book containing the lessons or lections—

	s.	d.
17 quires of vellum,	10	6
Writing,	25	0
9 skins and 1 quire (supplementary ?),	5	6
Writing,	3	2
Illuminating,	13	6
Binding in red skin,	5	5

In 1469, William Ebesham wrote out, among other

books, certain legal documents for 2*d*. a leaf,
probably in quarto, and Hoccleve's *De Regimine
Principum* for 3*s*. 9*d*., ' aftir a peny a leef, which is
right wele worth.'

It will not be out of place, in conclusion, to give
a few selected specimens of *colophons* or concluding
notes, in which the scribe's most inward mind at the
moment of the completion of his long task is often
revealed, whether the uppermost feeling be weari-
ness, malignity, religious feeling, expectancy, or
humour. An asterisk indicates one defective in
grammar or metre. The examples are arranged
roughly in order of the five feelings enumerated
above.

WEARINESS.

*Confer solamen et mentis tolle gravamen.
Judicis examen fac mite sit omnibus.   Amen.

Finis succrevit, manus et mea fessa quievit.

Finem scriptori liceat posuisse labori.

*Laus tibi sit, Christe, quoniam liber explicit iste :
Lassa manus calamusque simul cum fine quievit.

Hic scriptor cesso scribendo pollice fesso.

Scribere qui cupiunt, sensum Deus augeat illis.

MALIGNITY.

*Finito libro frangamus ossa magistro.

RELIGIOUS FEELING.

Sit laus scribenti, sit vita salusque legenti.

Hoc scribens carmen sit benedictus.   Amen.

Explicit iste liber : sit scriptor crimine liber.

Sor   sup   no   scrip   li   poci
     te   er   rum   tor bri   atur
Mor   inf   no   rap   li   mori

Finito libro reddatur gratia Christo.

Ne scribam vanum, duc, pia Virgo, manum.

Dextram scriptoris benedicat mater honoris :
    Duc pennam, rege cor, sancta Maria, precor.

O Mater Dei, memento mei.

Pennam scribentis benedicat lingua legentis.

EXPECTANCY.

Nunc finem feci : da mihi quod merui.

Librum scribendo complevi fine jocundo :
Promisso pretio sum dignus jure peracto.

Finem scriptori liceat posuisse labori,
Ast operis longi detur sibi munere fungi.

HUMOUR.

Nunc scripsi totum : pro Christo da mihi potum.

Vinum scriptori debetur de meliori.

*Explicit.—Expliceat !   Ludere scriptor eat.

*Heu male finivi quia scribere non bene scivi :
Scribere qui nescit dicit quod penna vilescit.

Jesus mercy, Lady helpe :
For Cutt my dogge is a parillus welp.

Explicit liber ; incipit pastus.

Omnibus est notum quod multum diligo potum :
Qui bona vina bibit Paradiso fortius ibit.

CHAPTER V

ILLUMINATIONS

THE set and traditional forms of letters allow so little scope for artistic variety, that however interesting the subject-matter of a manuscript may be, we sometimes feel a sense of disappointment and even of distaste as we turn the page of a bare written volume, in which the writing is perhaps to us not easily legible, and design and colour have no place. Our interest and pleasure is at least doubled when the setting of the record is itself beautiful. Even the red rubrics, the plain alternate blue and red letters common in headlines in the fourteenth century, relieve the eye ; but when the capital letters are floriated, when the margins are filled with leaf-and-branch work, and when every few pages exhibit a delicately painted miniature, some scene from the artist's own experience,—a market-place, it may be, with a housewife and loom within a doorway, a blacksmith at his forge, and the neigh-bours chaffering and bargaining in the open square, above which tower the town-hall and cathedral of his native town ; or some banquet at the court of Burgundy in the fifteenth century, with its parade of magnificence, the gorgeous hangings and crowds of long-slippered pages, but (as we should think) its essential discomfort ; or, again, a religious scene rivalling in effect and minuteness of detail the greater pictures of Italian artists,—then, indeed, we feel that the accessories have invested the written page with a beauty and attractiveness beyond the powers of a scribe alone. In this short chapter we can only touch on some striking points in the development of this fascinating art of illumination, till it reached its zenith in the last half of the fifteenth century.

The idea of ornamenting books in one way or another is as old as books themselves ; nevertheless, it is generally true that the earliest writing is the plainest and freest from accessory decoration ; thus the Herculanean Papyri, the Codex Alexandrinus in the British Museum, the Codex Amiatinus, show a minimum of colour ; and in the earliest MSS. there is nothing to mark even the beginning of a new sentence or chapter. The lines along which development took place were natural and simple. First, certain letters (usually the first letter of a new sentence, but sometimes the first letter of the line which *followed* the commencement of a sentence) were made simply larger than the rest, and perhaps coloured. Next, the ends and corners of such letters were exaggerated, and ran over into the margin, until in course of time the whole margin was filled with offshoots from one or more large letters. Lastly, the margin was formally separated from the letters, and received a wholly independent design. Meanwhile room was found, either within a letter, or about a margin, or in the text, or on a separate page, for a miniature, the highest form of illumination, which in the best examples rivals in completeness and power the finest paintings of picture galleries, though the scale is necessarily much smaller.

Before we treat of styles, we may premise something of the conditions and materials in which illuminators worked. The *illuminatores*, or monks set to the task of ornamenting books in a monastery, used the scriptorium in common with the scribes, and were hardly distinguished in discipline from the latter. The painters of miniatures, introducing elaborate scenes and human figures, must at all times have been treated with more respect than the designers of capital letters, marginal ornaments, rubrications, and headlines, and we often find two quite different hands on the same page, showing that the higher work (and remuneration) were reserved for special artists. It is very probable that by far the greatest amount of book-ornamentation was done in religious houses, especially in Benedictine and Dominican establishments. The evidence for this is not only the preponderance of religious subjects, but also that the name of nearly every miniaturist of importance, till say A.D. 1450, betokens either a monk or an artist working for ecclesiastical purposes.

The colours used—which were made with great care, as the numerous treatises on their preparation evince—were primarily gold, red, and blue, less commonly green, purple, yellow, white, and black. The only preparation which needs special description here is the gold. When we read of a *codex aureus* or *argenteus* (a manuscript in gold or silver), we must understand one in which, not the background, but the letters, are of those substances. And usually, especially about the time of Charles the Great, and, as a revival, in the fifteenth century, it will be found in such MSS., that to heighten the effect of these colours the whole leaf or leaves of parchment have been dyed a deep purple. The effect is extremely fine ; and not only gold, but red and white paint also show well on it. This dyeing is not often found between the periods mentioned above. Gold has been laid on in different ways at different times. It is a peculiar fact that it is not found at all in the British Isles before the tenth century. Until about the twelfth century it was laid on in powder, and always, if closely looked at, has a ruddy appearance. The description of a book as *aureis literis rutilans* (with a ruddy glow from its golden letters) precisely gives the impression to the eye. But after that century gold was laid on with extraordinary care, and burnished, producing the glittering effect we often see in mediæval illumination, in which a single page may contain more than a hundred separate and delicate pieces of burnished and shining gold. First, a peculiar light pink clay, which was often brought from the East, and much prized in monasteries, was placed on the parchment, after the design had been drawn in outline ; then size was laid on it, next gold-leaf, and, finally, the gold was burnished by hand with an agate. This one would naturally expect to be done before other colours were laid on, since otherwise the rough action of rubbing would spoil the surrounding part ; and it is actually proved by the not infrequent occurrence of an unfinished book, in which the design is found extending farthest in the volume, the clay next, and the burnished gold some pages later than the last occurrence of other colours.

Styles of Illumination

1. *The Early Period.*—We have no examples of classical illumination left : nothing whatever, in fact, from classical times except descriptions of, or allusions to, the art of painting books in classical authors. The nearest approaches we can make are in the Pompeian wall-paintings, and the coloured wooden mummy cases from Egypt. But we have very early MSS. with paintings quite clearly based on classical models as known from sculpture. The two early MSS. of Virgil in the Vatican, and the famous *Iliad* in the Ambrosian Library at Milan, will serve as examples, all being not later than the fourth century of our era. The characteristics of these are simplicity and directness in aim, with no straining after effect, and few accessories ; plenty of colour, but very little shading. It may be said that

ornamented borders and elaborate initial letters are quite rare. The background is often an olive green, and the border is noticeable, consisting of a plain band or bands of colour carried as a rectangle round the picture, sometimes with gold lozenges. The faces and poses are those with which we are familiar in classical statues and coins. The Ashburnham Pentateuch (now restored to Paris) is a good example of the style as produced on the Continent in the seventh century, the ' dark age ' of arts and literature in every part of Europe except Ireland. In this particular case, though the art can only be called debased, the brilliance of the colours and boldness of design make it a magnificent volume, and one of the last of the grander examples of the classical style. This survival of the style till the time of Charles the Great is the one great feature of early illuminations. But there was another element which affected the whole of Europe—the Byzantine—as especially seen in the almost universal type of the Evangelists. The pose of the figure, the chair, the footstool, the writing-desk, and bookstand, are of the Byzantine or Greek kind, and constantly recur in European MSS. of the Early and Mediæval Periods.

2. *First Mediæval Period.*—This begins in Ireland in the sixth, and on the Continent in the eighth century, when we first find ornaments and designs independent of Roman style, although the famous Terences of the Vatican and the National Library at Paris show that the older kind survived for many

years later. Its close may be placed in the thirteenth century. Ireland leads the way, although every product of the school of ornamentation which must have existed in the sixth century has perished. Still, the earliest Irish MS. we know, the Cathach Psalter, written in about A.D. 600, already exhibits at least two of the peculiarities of the Irish and (later) Hiberno-Saxon school—the rows of red dots round a design, and the dragon's head. It is in the second half of the seventh century that we find the Book of Kells, the glory of Trinity College, Dublin. The taste and delicacy, the originality, the elaboration of the colouring and design, place it among the wonders of the world. Among the other peculiarities of the style—the origin of which is still a matter of dispute —are the Z-patterns (fine lines arranged diagonally, like natural and reversed Zeds combined); interlaced ribbon-work; a profusion of monstrous forms of birds, snakes, lizards, and hounds, generally extravagantly elongated and knotted; and certain spiral forms given off from a central point, and each in turn giving off an adjacent spiral, the general type being invariably a combination of C-shapes, and never of S-forms. But the limitations of excellence are also obvious. When the human figure or historical scenes are attempted, the effect is poor and often barbarous, and even trees and flowers were avoided by Irish artists; so that our judgment on the Irish school must be that it exhibits, not the highest form of art, but the highest development of

that particular grade of art in which regularity and
minuteness (what may be called geometrical ingenuity) hold a more important place than free
drawing from nature.

As it is hard to find any certain antecedents of
Irish art, so it is hard to find any succeeding continental ornamentation free from Irish influence. It
was, as Sir E. Maunde Thompson says, ' the origin of
the systems of illumination which sprang up on the
Continent, and notably of the Carlovingian.' The
influence of Charles the Great on handwriting (see
p. 28) was hardly greater than on the style of ornamentation, so that the Irish school contributed very
largely through Alcuin (*d*. 804) to the style of the
one great continental school of the time. But if
this is true of the ornament, it was the classical school
which supplied the study of the human figure, and
again it was the Byzantine which is to be traced in
certain parts of the border (such as the arcade and
many of the architectural details), and in the
extended use of gold. It is now that we first find
books lavishly and systematically embellished. The
Carolingian style may be said to have died out in the
tenth century.

In the period from A.D. 900 to 1250 we find several
well-marked tendencies. The form of the letter is
regarded less and the painting more, so that we find
designs actually obscuring the underlying shape ;
the border is no longer straight and plain, but
freer, and with architectural or other design. The

miniature grows from a single figure to a scene of more or less complexity. A scene within a letter is not found earlier than the eleventh century. There is a well-known type of Latin Bible found especially in French and English work, in the twelfth and thirteenth centuries, showing usually a minute hand, double columns in a page, and initial letters which are coloured with straight, stiff outline, very long, and with divisions and geometrical designs or medalions within these stiff bounding lines; blue and red being the prevailing colours, with some gold.

There are some curious points in the comparative development of national styles. On the Continent, the hundred years nearest to A.D. 1000 are years of small progress in the art of illumination; but in England that same period produces a truly national style, neither Irish nor continental. There is outline drawing of figures with exaggerated hands and feet, elaborate but formal drapery, and an unmistakable cast of countenance. Late in the eleventh century this style dies out in England under continental influence, and sometimes we can see the two forces almost equally balanced in a single manuscript. In fact, from the Norman Conquest to A.D. 1200, English style is hardly found; but the seesaw, so to say, with the Continent is still preserved, for just at that time the French, Italian and German national styles are forming.

From about 1300 to about 1350 there is a distinctive East Anglian school of high excellence, which

is seen at its best in four Psalters, in the British
Museum, Bodleian, Dyson Perrin's and Fitzwilliam
(Cambridge) libraries, and known as the Arundel,
Ormesby, Gorleston and St. Omer Psalters.
The style cannot here be described in detail,
but several illustrations will be found in S. C.
Cockerell's *Gorleston Psalter*, 1907. Some authorities
claim this period as the brightest in the history of
English illumination, in view not only of this
special school, but of such magnificent MSS. as
Queen Mary's Psalter, one of the great treasures of
the British Museum both for the beauty and the
extent of its illuminations.

3. *The best Period* (A.D. 1250-1550).—Probably the
finest examples of illumination are to be found in the
fifteenth century in France, Italy, England, and the
Netherlands, though some still prefer the costly,
magnificent and florid ornamentation of the first
quarter of the sixteenth century. The art is,
however, generally in decline after about A.D. 1480.

This latest period of European art, from A.D. 1250
onward, is as well marked by the progress of the
border as by any single feature. First we find a
letter, pure and simple, within the limits of the
written page, with the exception of a simple ex-
crescence, like a pendant, encroaching on the
margin, as in the French Bibles, described on p. 63.
Next, the pendant grows to a leafy branch ; and
even by the end of the thirteenth century we may
find this branch running completely round the text,

either as a narrow formal stem, usually painted in two colours, with a few angular leaves; or more artistically treated as a natural branch, with leaves and animals or grotesques intertwined among the boughs. But still the border grows out of the initial letter, and is not substantial and complete in itself. Next, in the fourteenth century we find this stem becoming a solid border, throwing out leaves and buds, and making itself almost a separate thing, though still formally growing out of the letter. The excessive use of blue and red, alternate or in any combination, is a general mark of this period. Lastly, when we come to the fifteenth century, the border becomes wholly detached from the initial letter, and indeed is often the work of a different hand. Now it is distinct, the border is treated separately in various ways, shortly to be described, while fruit, birds, butterflies, and flowers, drawn from nature, abound.

Two specially English coloured ornaments may be noticed as belonging to fourteenth century art : a tassel-ornament of red hair lines, with green freely used in the body ; and a border of stem and leaves, throwing off thin twisted tendrils with gold balls at end, a characteristic shared with Italy which lasted till the middle of the fifteenth century. With respect to the miniatures of the period, except for a set-back during the second half of the fourteenth century in England, we find a general advance from formality to the truest study of inanimate and

F

animate nature, ending with veritable pictures. One
test of this advance is appreciation of the principles
of perspective ; for not till after the beginning of the
fifteenth century do we find true perspective
throughout the picture. In the fourteenth and
fifteenth centuries France and (within France) Paris
are *facile principes* in the art of illumination, and a
few designs, found chiefly in French art, may be
mentioned. In the former century a favourite
background is formed by a diaper or diamond
pattern of alternate colours, blue and red, or blue
and gold. In the next century we find at least four
general kinds of fine French work : *floriated*, where
flowers and birds are painted in natural arrangement ; *ivy-leaf*, when stems are found, thin or thick,
throwing out ivy leaves of gold or other colour with
some tendrils (see Plate VI.) ; *line and leaf*, where
the stem is a hair line only, but still enters into the
design as an integral part, the leaves being as in the
preceding style ; and *geometrical*, in which the whole
border is divided into pieces by symmetrical lines,
each piece being separately filled up with ornament.
German art is singularly heavy and formal, and if we
judge by style, about one century behind the rest of
Western Europe in development at each period.
Italian is the most vigorous and marked style after
French and English, and in many ways follows the
lines of its schools of painting. In it until the
fourteenth century borders seem hardly to be used
as an artistic feature at all ; marked characteristics

PLATE VI : St. MICHAEL. (1407, French).

after A.D. 1300 are a small gold disc with tendrils radiating from it, and white bands interlacing in the old Irish style.

It is hoped that these few and vague words on a subject which cannot be properly treated without more detail and without coloured illuminations, may suggest lines of investigation to be followed out as opportunity offers : see a list of selected works on the subject in Appendix C.

CHAPTER VI

THE ERRORS OF SCRIBES AND THEIR CORRECTION

Textual Criticism

THE object of most of the work bestowed at the present day on manuscripts is to discover and edit new literary or historical treasures, or to restore the actual words as written by an ancient author, by the exercise of a trained intellect on the more or less faulty materials which have survived to the present time. When we consider how liable a copyist is to errors of transcription, and how, when once an error has been made and has escaped correction, it cannot but be repeated by the next copyist, who also introduces his own new ones, and that in the course of centuries this process of deterioration is theoretically accelerated, and complicated by irresponsible attempts at conjectural emendation, we cease to wonder at the importance and honour accorded to Textual Criticism, the system by which the sources of error are classified, and an attempt is made to reverse the course of depravation and undo the accumulated perversions of many generations.

The textual critic then keeps chiefly before him the mind and the hand of the scribe, to which alone can be due variations from the original authentic

text ; and in this spirit he considers the manuscripts
of his author to which he has access, trying to
separate them into classes, according to the
peculiarities which they display. He may prove
that several of them point back to a single older
manuscript, from which they were all derived, and
which in relation to these later copies is called their
archetype. By this conclusion he has mounted one
step nearer to the author's original text ; and if he
can discern several archetypes of existing groups of
MSS., he may compare even these phantom arche-
typal MSS., and so penetrate farther and farther
into the mist of ages. This is the principle of
Genealogy, and may be illustrated by a few simple
examples. (1) The *Discourses* of Arrian, based on
the teaching of his master Epictetus, called the
Διατριβαὶ Ἐπικτήτου, were written in the second
century after Christ, and exhibit the highest point
which Stoic philosophy ever reached. But no MS.
of them exists which is older than the twelfth century. In book I. 18. 9 of the *Discourses* there is a
passage of which all the printed editions and all the
MSS. make a hash ; some omit the passage, some
print words which make no sense, and some indicate
by blanks that they cannot deal with the difficulty.
But in one MS. alone, the oldest, there is at this very
passage a curious oval smear in the middle of the
page, which on investigation accounts for all the
vagaries of other MSS. and editions. We cannot
possibly doubt that this MS. is the archetype of all

other existing copies of the *Discourses*.   It is seldom, however, that so clear and decisive a proof can be found.   (2) In a MS. of mediæval letters there is one which begins, ' Frater Æ. pauperum Christi ' (brother Æ[thelredus], one of the poor of Christ).   This is quite straightforward ;   but in one MS. nearly contemporary with the writer himself, the letter begins, ' Frater *de* pauperum Christi,' which cannot be translated.   A comparison of several MSS. shows that the *de* is a mistake by an ignorant scribe, who mistook a peculiar form of Æ for *de*.   Now, whenever a MS. is found with *de*, we may feel pretty sure that such a peculiar blunder would not twice be made, and that any second later occurrence of the word is due to a copyist who had the first blunderer's own copy before him, and was unable or (we may hope) unwilling to attempt to restore the text by any conjecture of his own.   (3) A master-mind like Traube's could do even more than this.   As Professor W. M. Lindsay says, ' At one touch of Traube's magic wand the Berne MS. [of Valerius Maximus] has become one of the most precious monuments of mediæval learning.'   Traube established the fact that it had been transcribed for Servatus Lupus, the great literary light of ninth-century France, that it was copied from an exemplar written probably at Fulda by an English or Irish scribe, and that that scribe had before him a codex written in capitals !

But when errors are not so easily traced, as in the

second example, the textual critic is allowed to consider, not only the mind and the hand of the scribe, but also (and, so to speak, on his own responsibility) the mind of the author also. It is, however, a very slippery matter when one argues from general style, or from similar passages found elsewhere in the work, that the author must have written such and such words ; and the tendency of modern criticism is to confine the use of parallel passages to illustration or corroboration, and to deprecate that attractive exercise of ingenuity which suggests readings not found in any existing manuscript (' Conjectural Emendation '),—except within narrow limits, such as when a great author is only preserved to us in a few manuscripts (perhaps one only), as is the case with Catullus and part of the *Annals* of Tacitus.

It is a remarkable fact that instead of the corruptions and variations increasing in number in proportion to the distance of MSS. from the author's time, that number after a time seems not merely not to increase indefinitely, as might be expected, but actually to diminish ; partly from the correction of blunders by too intelligent scribes, partly from what is called ' mixture ' of MSS., one copy being used to correct and remove the faults of another, so that eccentricities of a single copyist are gradually eliminated by his successors through a comparison of other codexes.

We will now give a classification of sources of error in transcription, and a list of the chief principles on which these errors are corrected.

I. Sources of Error in Transcription

A. Unintelligent.—1. *Errors of sight* or hearing. —These occur when the eye of the scribe (or, in the less usual case of dictation, the ear) fails to grasp correctly what has to be copied. A common error is for a whole line of the MS. which is being copied to drop out ; and usually the cause of it is that two lines end with the same word or termination, and the scribe's eye has slipped over the first to the second one. Suppose part of the Lord's Prayer written in old style, with no stops or capitals, thus :—

> bethynamethy
> kingdomcomethy
> willbedonein.

a copyist might easily omit altogether the second line, because of the Homoioteleuton, as it is called, which might cause the eye to slip from the first *thy* to the second. Probably no Greek MS. of the New Testament is free from an example of this.

2. *Errors of memory*.—These occur when, in the interval between seeing and writing, some unconscious cerebration takes place in the copyist's head, and he puts down something wrong. Parallel passages are a very common source of mistake, when the copyist remembers another set of words similar, but

not identical, with that before him, and blunders.
Thus, in Virgil's *Æn*. vii. 324, the copyist of an early
MS. probably had *ab sede dearum* before him, but
was misled by a recollection of *Æn*. vii. 454 (where
MSS. do not differ) to put down *ab sede sororum*,
which is now found in many MSS., and almost no
editions. The point is, that it is so unlikely that a
copyist would introduce *dearum* out of his own head,
whereas he might easily introduce *sororum* wrongly,
if he was well acquainted with his Virgil.

3. *Errors of intellect.*—In Latin, the contraction
$\overline{mr}$ stands for both *mater* and *martyr*, and $\overline{mia}$
stands for both *miseria* and *misericordia*. It might
easily happen that a copyist would unintelligently
expand some such contraction wrongly.

B. INTELLIGENT.—1. *Incorporation of marginal
glosses or various readings.*—Often when a word or
passage is difficult, it is glossed by the scribe or by
the reader ; that is to say, something is written just
over it, or in the margin, to make it clearer. In
Shakespeare's time the word ' owe ' had a meaning
to ' own ' ; we can therefore imagine a copy of
Shakespeare in which ' to him that owes it ' might be
glossed by ' owns.' Some later copyist, say a
foreigner, could easily be conceived as writing, ' to
him that owes owns it,' thus incorporating the gloss,
because he did not understand it, and thought it to
be an addition accidentally omitted, and by all
means to be inserted. So, in old days, when one
MS. was compared with another, it was a custom to

write a variation on the margin of one of the two, and this might be similarly incorporated.

2. *Correction of apparent difficulties*, such as unusual forms and expressions, seeming contradictions, or incomplete quotations. Unfortunately, the tendency to make a text read well by removing difficulties led scribes in uncritical times to substitute, with no deliberate desire to mislead, easy words for archaic, and plain for obscure.

3. *Deliberate falsification*, such as a change of a theological text for dogmatic reasons. In ordinary MSS., even where there might be temptation, this fault is quite rare ; but a curious example may probably be found in Virgil, see p. 79.

II. PRINCIPLES ON WHICH TRANSCRIPTIONAL ERRORS ARE CORRECTED

In the following list the principles are in italics, followed by a brief explanation, if necessary, and references (1) to the foregoing sources of error, and (2) to passages in Virgil which may be taken as examples, if recourse be had to a critical edition such as Conington's or Ribbeck's ; but let it be understood that the passages are only adduced to show how a single principle operates in practice, for it is not suggested that that single principle in each case leads to the best text, since it may be overborne by still weightier considerations of another kind.

1. *A short reading is to be preferred to one more verbose.* This is due to the tendency of scribes to

incorporate glosses, to expand hard phrases by easier
ones which are often longer, and often to a conscien-
tious desire to put into the text all there is in the
MS. copied, whether glosses or various readings or
corrections (B. 1, B. 2).

Æn. ii. 778 :—

$$\text{Nec te } \begin{cases} \text{hinc comitem asportare} \\ \text{comitem hinc asportare} \\ \text{comitem asportare} \end{cases} \text{Creüsam | Fas.}$$

(Nor is it right for you to bear hence with you Creüsa.)

Here the *hinc*, which is found both before and
after *comitem*, and is in some MSS. omitted, excites
suspicion that it is a gloss which has crept into the
text ; and when we see how apposite as a gloss the
word would be (to show that *asportare*, ' to carry
off,' is quite distinct from *apportare*, ' to carry to '),
our suspicion is increased. In fact, we can hardly
doubt that the third line above is the right text, and
that the shorter reading is to be preferred. But
how soon the *hinc* found its way into the text may be
judged from the fact that Servius, the early commentator on Virgil, declares that the common
reading in his time (the fifth century ?) could not be
scanned ; so clearly his text was No. 2 in the
parallel readings at the head of this note. Another
example of this principle will be found in *Æn.* vii.
464, 465. The whole principle has been forcibly
challenged by Professor A. C. Clark, who has found
that accidental omissions are more numerous and
more important than have been suspected, but his

criticism affects sentences and complete lines rather than words or expressions.

2. *A difficult or obscure reading is better than one which is*, from the point of view of the copyist, *fuller and easier* (B. 2).

Æn. xi. 708 :—

Iam nosces, ventosa ferat cui gloria $\begin{cases} \text{fraudem.} \\ \text{laudem.} \\ \text{pœnam.} \end{cases}$

(Quickly you shall know to which side wind-blown fame will bring defeat.)

This is a good example of a difficult reading (difficult to the mind of the scribe) being preferable. *Fraus*, which seems at first sight impossible to translate, since there is no idea of deceit in the passage, had in early Latin the sense of injury, and here means harm, defeat. But copyists who did not know this old meaning substituted *laudem*, ' victory,' and some who did know it glossed it by *pœnam*, which subsequent copyists took, not as a gloss, but as a better reading. Obviously we should prefer *fraudem.* *Æn.* i. 636 is in some points a similar case.

3. *A less emphatic reading is nearer to the original text* (B. 2). No author is always at his best, and few writings cannot be improved by persons far inferior to the writer. The common quotation, *Sic volo, sic jubeo : stet pro ratione voluntas*, a forcible line, ought to be given in the weaker but more correct form, *Hoc volo, sic jubeo : sit . . .* (Juvenal).

Æn. vi. 664 :—

Quique sui memores $\begin{Bmatrix} \text{aliquos} \\ \text{alios} \end{Bmatrix}$ fecere merendo.

(And who by their good deeds made some to remember them.)

Aliquos is undoubtedly weak ; so weak that Conington declares *alios* (others) to be ' infinitely preferable,' since it introduces some little antithesis between ' themselves ' and ' others.' But *aliquos* has decidedly the better testimony, and Virgil probably let a careless line escape him.

4. *Readings which owe their origin to simple carelessness on the part of the scribe are rightly rejected* (A. 1-3).

Æn. ix. 657 :—

Apollo | Mortales medio $\begin{Bmatrix} \text{aspectu} \\ \text{aspectus} \end{Bmatrix}$ sermone relinquit.

(Apollo vanishes from mortal sight before his words are ended.)

|The extraordinary circumstance about this line is that *all* the leading MSS. (three uncials and the chief cursive) read *aspectu*, which makes nonsense of the passage (' Apollo leaves mortals, while looking at them, with a remark ! '). In fact, a reading which has by far the best support is entirely given up by editors, because due to an early scribal blunder. The excuse for its existence at all is, of course, that *medio* precedes, and a word beginning with *s* follows, so that MEDIOASPECTUSSERMONE was, as it were, a trap for the inattentive.

5. *Out of several readings, that one is best which*

lies apparently midmost among the others.   It is very
instructive, when a passage is beset with variations
in the MSS., to attempt to reconstruct the Scala
Vitiorum, and make a probable genealogy of the
readings, whether blunders or corrections.   The
one which will best account for all the others, and
with which the others can be most easily causally
connected, is probably the right one (A. and B.).

Æn. ix. 632-4 :—

```
' Sagitta | . . . venit et cava tempora ferro
  Transigit.  " I,
  Transadigit.
  Traicit.     " I,  ⎬ verbis virtutem illude superbis." '
  Transiit.    " I,
  Traiecit.
```

(The arrow flies and pierces the hollow temples [of Remulus]
with iron barb. ' Go to, now mock my valour with thy vaunts.')

The first four readings above are those of the three
uncials and the chief cursive MS. which contain the
passage.   The fifth is the corrected reading of the
same cursive, and is found also in inferior MSS.
Now, what is the pedigree of corruption, and
which the form from which the error first sprang ?
The ' I,' if not recognized as a complete word
by itself, would naturally cause some confusion
(TRAICITIVERBIS), and also the form *traicio*
instead of the longer *trans-icio*.   The probable
genealogy would seem on the whole to be one which
selects *traicit i* as the ' midmost ' reading from which
the rest have most naturally sprung :—

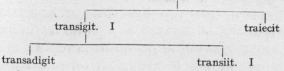

But there must have been considerable variation even before our existing MSS. were written.

6. *Omissions may be suspected when the passages wanting are repugnant to natural feeling or orthodox belief* (B. 3).

Æn. ii. 567-588.

This is a well-known passage, in which the hero of the *Æneid* discusses with himself whether he shall slay Helen in cold blood. The omission of the passage, whether by Tucca and Varius (see next page) or in some very early MS., is an argument for their genuineness, when we consider how shocking the idea must have seemed even to Roman minds. Most editors enclose them in brackets as doubtful, but they would appear to be genuine.

We may continue this chapter with two specimens of the literary history of famous books, selected because the amount of testimony to them, both in the number and importance of their MSS., is greater than of any other ancient authors whatever—Virgil and the Four Gospels.

1. *Virgil (Publius Vergilius Maro)*

It is recorded of Virgil, as of Tennyson, that he wrote much more than he published, and that he was

occupied for much of his time in cutting down and
reducing to their best form passages thrown off in
the heat of composition.   Even at the end of his life
he was so diffident of the merits of the *Æneid* that
he wished to burn it.   It appears to be certain that
Virgil himself wrote out his poems in their best
form ; for Aulus Gellius, in the second century of
our era, distinctly records that he saw the autograph
original manuscript of the Georgics.   After Virgil's
death, in B.C. 19, Tucca and Varius published,
according to their discretion, the *Æneid ;* and even
at this time may have removed from the text the
lines in the second book (567-588), in which, as has
just been said, the hero of the work expresses his
deliberate desire to put Helen to death.   Servius
preserves the lines, and they occur in the text of
only a few late MSS.   Publication would, of course,
mean that scribes were allowed to copy the autograph of Virgil, and that these transcripts were
themselves copied, and the process continued till
the invention of printing.   Our oldest existing MSS.
of the *Æneid* are the following : The Palatine (P),
in the Vatican at Rome, of the third or fourth
century ; the Vatican (R = Romanus), perhaps of
the same date, and adorned with nineteen remarkable pictures illuminated in a classical style ; the
Medicean (known as M), in the Laurentian Library
at Florence, of the fifth century ; and three sets of
fragments, in the Vatican (F, perhaps of the third
century, still containing no less than fifty miniatures

of the greatest interest and value), at St. Gall (G), and at Verona (V, a palimpsest [1]). All these are in capitals, chiefly rustic capitals, and are followed by a host of minuscule MSS., from the ninth century onwards, which have never been enumerated at length, but must amount to two or three hundred at least.

2. *The Four Gospels*

It is generally agreed that after the death of Christ the history of His life and doctrine was carried on by oral tradition only, with no written record. But as soon as persecution began to disperse the Christians, it was inevitable that for fear of unconscious distortion, or even of simple forgetfulness of the facts, some record should be made which could be put in the hands of disciples departing to distant lands ; it was the only possible way of preventing hopeless disagreement, or incomplete exposition of their common doctrine. In this way, no doubt, originated the four histories now known as the Gospels. The earliest testimony we have to the text is contained in the writings of the early Fathers, where they quote passages from, or otherwise describe, the history of

---

[1] A *palimpsest* (from παλίμψηστος, *palimpsēstos*, scraped again) is a MS. from which the old writing has been as far as possible scraped to allow of the parchment being again used for later writing. In the British Museum (MS. Add. 17,212) is a rare example of a double palimpsest. Lowest is an uncial MS. of the 5th cent., containing a fragment of the *Annales* of C. Granius Licinianus ; next, a grammatical Latin treatise, in cursive minuscule ; and on the top a Syriac translation of Chrysostom's Homilies, itself not later than the ninth or tenth century !

Christ ; and it is in accordance with the course of events described above that we find in the earliest notices a real but not a verbal agreement with our present text. Soon, however, the agreement becomes close, and we can see that the reference is to standard written accounts. The next earliest class of witness to the text is, strange to say, that of versions or translations. There is evidence, for instance, of a Syriac version of the Gospels in the second century ; of an Egyptian, two forms of which are quite possibly also of the second century ; a Latin in the third century ; a Gothic, by Bishop Ulfilas, certainly of the fourth century ; and Æthiopic and Armenian versions before A.D. 600.

Lastly, we come to the age of our existing MSS. of the Greek Text. Two are ascribed to the fourth century ; one, the *Codex Sinaiticus* (known as ℵ, Aleph), the romantic discovery of which is related on p. III, a MS. of the whole Bible in Greek, now imperfect, but still containing the whole of the New Testament, written (and it is unique in this respect) with four columns on a page ; the other, the *Codex Vaticanus* (B), also when perfect a MS. of the whole Bible, written in three columns, one of the chief treasures of the Vatican at Rome. Next in point of age ranks the *Codex Alexandrinus* (A), probably written in the fifth century, a complete Bible, presented to Charles I. in 1628 by Cyril Lucar, Patriarch of Constantinople, he having obtained it from Alexandria, of which he had been Patriarch,

and where it had rested for many centuries.
George II. placed it in the British Museum, with
his library, in 1757, and it has ever since been its
chief manuscript treasure. To the fifth century also
belongs the *Codex rescriptus Ephraëmi* (C), in the
National Library at Paris, once a Bible, now a
collection of fragments containing about two-thirds
of its original contents. It is a palimpsest, the
ancient writing, after being scraped, bearing above
it some Greek works of Ephrem Syrus, written in the
twelfth century. *Codex Bezæ* (D), containing the
Gospels and Acts (nearly complete), and originally
the Catholic Epistles, in Greek and Latin, is the
glory of the Cambridge University Library, and is
generally ascribed to the sixth century. It was
presented to the University in 1581 by Theodorus
Beza, who obtained it from the monastery of St.
Irenæus at Lyons, after it was sacked in 1562. It
is celebrated for the extraordinary variations from
and additions to the received text, but the most
recent critics attach a high value to its readings.

All the five above-mentioned MSS. are written on
fine vellum, in quarto form, with uncial letters. In
all, there are twenty-one uncial Greek MSS. of the
Gospels, or, counting fragments, sixty-six, each of
which is known among scholars by a capital letter,
or, in the case of fragments, by a capital letter
together with a small letter : the majority belong to
the sixth, seventh, eighth, and ninth centuries.
This list is succeeded by a multitude of later MSS. in

minuscule writing, the number of which, for the Gospels alone, is at least 1300, ranging from the ninth to the seventeenth century.

The number of witnesses to the text of Virgil and the Four Gospels is so great, that conjectural emendation is, in fact, not allowable for either book. And this superabundance has also its use when we have to consider less fortunate authors like Lucan or Propertius ; for we are able, by surveying the body of New Testament MSS., to estimate fairly the relation of late to early copies in point of accuracy and general worth, and to confirm our general confidence in a text even when no early testimony to it has survived.

Curiosities of Palæography

At this point it may be allowable to lighten the subject of scribal errors by some examples of unusual or humorous results of their mistakes. The first place may be taken by *Ghost Words*— words entirely due to blunders. Every museum contains some ' celts,' or flint implements, a word which first appears about A.D. 1700. It appears that there is no Celtic connexion in the word, but that it arose from a misunderstanding of the Vulgate of Job xix. 23-24. ' Quis mihi det ut (sermones mei) exarentur in libro . . . vel *celte* sculpantur in silice ? ' *Celte* was taken as an ablative from a supposed *celtis*, an engraving instrument, but it is really a phonetic variant of the adverb ' certe ' (certainly, ' permanently,' as the Hebrew and the Septuagint) !

The resemblance of the strokes or pot-hooks which make up *m, n, u* and *i* in mediæval writing (and even in early printing), especially when *i*'s had no dot and *v* was written *u*, is responsible for much. Not only can eight Latin words be made out of fifteen such strokes (*immuniui, innuimini, inunimini, minimum, munimini, numinum,nummum,* and *uiminium*), but the confusion has invaded our own *Te Deum,* where ' Make them to be numbered with Thy Saints in glory everlasting ' is due to mis-reading the Latin *munerari* (' Make them to be awarded with Thy Saints Thy glory everlasting ') as *numerari.* Till the last few years every loyal member of the Church of England was bidden to commemorate on September 7 a certain bishop Enurchus. No such bishop occurs in any Mar-tyrology, and it turns out that the word ' Euurci, (the genitive of Evurtius in mediæval writing) was misprinted *Enurchi* in the Preces Privatæ of 1564, and so caused the error. September 7 was Queen Elizabeth's birthday, and in 1604, when the ghostly saint first appears, no better known saint than Evurtius bishop of Orleans could be found on whom to base a commemoration of that day. That is the plausible suggestion made in the *Church Times* of September 1, 1905, by the Rev. Vernon Staley. It is perhaps ungallant to call attention to the fact that the lady who wrote the *Antiquities of*

Langharne (1871) after some years' residence in the town which she describes, found it necessary to head the list of Errata with the following notice :—
' For *Langharne* wherever it occurs, read *Laugharne*' ! ! In the second edition (1880) all is put right. Among other ghost-words are Grampian, Hebrides, St. Parasceve, Siatoutanda (see p. 147), Dedalricus (in German histories), and the commonest of all Roman praenomens, Caius !

The following may be taken as examples of *remarkable blunders*. The old way of writing MSS. without spaces between words caused even Virgil to make some odd mistakes. In Ecl. viii. 58, as a climax of impossibility he writes, ' Omnia vel medium fiant mare ' (' Let everything become mid ocean '), but the expression is peculiar and not obviously apt. He no doubt took the Greek expression, πάντα δ' ἔναλλα γένοιτο (' May everything be different '), and read ΕΝΑΛΛΑ as ΕΝΑΛΙΑ (' sea things ') ! That he was capable of this may be seen from Georg. i. 277 (Orcus), and Æn. ix. 716 (Inarime). All English Bibles of the Authorized Version of 1611 have perpetuated up to the present day the expression, ' Woe to the idol shepherd ! ' in Zech. xi. 17—a mere misprint for *idle :* and they all still present a hopeless error in Heb. x. 23, where the word ' faith ' (' Let us hold fast the profession of our faith ') is given as a translation of ἐλπίς, which is ' hope ' ! The name of Jervaulx Abbey (usually pronounced ' Jarvis '), on the Ure, is not obviously connected with Uredale, but the Latin name of the latter, Jorevallis, supplies the connexion. The signature of the Bishop of Salisbury (' —Sarum ') is based on an error. The scribe of the Middle Ages abbreviated all common words, and in a Salisbury roll or document would write Sar' (for Sarisburia or Sarisburiensis), just as Oxon' would imply Oxonia (Oxford) or Oxoniensis. Earlier, it would be written Sar/, or more commonly Sa𝔲, using an old shape of the *r*. But this shape of *r* plus the bar of Suspension (/) together make up the symbol No. vii. on p. 37, and the word was therefore (quite wrongly) re-expanded as Sarum !

CHAPTER VII

FAMOUS LIBRARIES

OF the libraries of ancient times very little is certainly known. Statements like that of Strabo, that Aristotle was the first collector of a library, add nothing to our knowledge, until we know more of the exact sense in which the words are used, and of the extent of what is here called a ' library ' ; while the library of clay tablets found at Nineveh, perhaps dating from the seventh century B.C., out of which some 20,000 are now in the British Museum, hardly comes under a description of manuscripts. The one great bibliothecarial fact of antiquity is the Library of Alexandria, founded by Ptolemy Soter (about B.C. 300), and the earliest recorded librarian of it was Zenodotus of Ephesus (about B.C. 280). The lowest computation of its size is 100,000 rolls. But of the three or four separate libraries at Alexandria under the Ptolemys, we cannot tell which were burnt in the time of Julius Cæsar and which survived till their destruction in or before the fourth century of the Christian era. One thing is certain, that if the Caliph Omar in A.D. 638 burnt any books in Alexondria (with the well-known decision that if the books in it were unorthodox they were pernicious,

and if orthodox, they must be superfluous), he did
not burn the ancient and famous library, for that
had perished long before his time. In Italy, we read
of extensive private libraries of Varro, Atticus, and
others ; but the only one about which we are on
sure ground is the private library found in the
eighteenth century at Herculaneum, after being
overwhelmed by the Vesuvian eruption of A.D. 79,
of which at least 350 rolls have been recovered by
excavation, and are, for the most part, preserved at
Naples (see p. 109). The earliest public library in
Rome is stated to have been built by Caius Asinius
Pollio on the Aventine, and the next is the Octavian
Library founded by the Emperor Augustus, B.C. 33.

As literature was never a prominent feature in
early monastic life, except in Ireland, so the library
of a religious house was, till mediæval times, a
subordinate part of the buildings. As has been
already mentioned, it is in the great houses of the
Benedictine Order that we find the largest libraries,
such as in England at Bury St. Edmund's, Glastonbury, Peterborough, Reading, St. Alban's, and,
above all, that of Christ Church in Canterbury,
perhaps the earliest library formed in England.
Among the other English monasteries of the libraries
of which we still possess catalogues or other details,
are St. Peter's at York, described in the eighth
century by Alcuin, St. Cuthbert's at Durham, and
St. Augustine's at Canterbury. At the dissolution
of the monasteries many libraries were dispersed,

and the basis of the great modern libraries is the
volumes thus scattered over England.

In early (classical) times papyrus rolls were kept
in horizontal pigeon-holes or in a pipe-like cylindrical
box (*capsa*). Volumes in book form lay flat in the
cupboard (*armarium*), and this custom lasted into
mediæval times (see Plate IV). But in general,
from Charles the Great's time onwards, the volumes
were disposed much as now, that is to say, upright,
and in large cases affixed to a wall, often with doors.
The larger volumes at least were in many cases
chained, so that they could only be used within
about six feet of their proper place ; and since the
chain was always riveted on the fore-edge of one of
the sides of a book, the back of the volume had to
be thrust first into the shelf, leaving the front edge
of the leaves exposed to view. Many old volumes
bear a mark in ink on this front edge ; and when this
is the case we may be sure that it was once chained
in a library ; and usually a little further investigation will disclose the mark of a rivet on one of the
sides. There are still some old libraries in which all
or some of the MSS. are chained, as at Hereford
Cathedral, Wimborne Minster, and Merton College,
Oxford. Regulations were carefully made to prevent the mixture of different kinds of books, and
their overcrowding or inconvenient position ; while
an organized system of lending was in vogue, by
which at least once a year, and less formally at
shorter intervals, the monks could change or renew

the volumes already on loan. Richard de Bury,
Bishop of Durham in the fourteenth century, when
framing rules for the library of a hall at Oxford to
which he intended to leave his manuscripts, insisted
that only ' duplicates ' should be lent to students
outside the hall, and then only after a ' caution ' or
pledge had been deposited which exceeded the
volume in value, and after a memorandum had been
made of the circumstances. But to students of the
hall his books were to be lent freely, on condition
that they were exhibited yearly to the custodians of
his library.

Let us take an example of the arrangement of a
monastic library of no special distinction in A.D.
1400,—that at Titchfield Abbey,—describing it in
the words of the register of the monastery itself, only
translating the Latin into English. ' The arrangement of the library of the monastery of Tychefeld
is this :—There are in the library of Tychefeld four
cases (*columnæ*) in which to place books, of which
two, the first and second, are on the eastern wall ;
on the southern wall is the third, and on the northern
wall the fourth. And each of them has eight shelves
(*gradus*), marked with a letter and number affixed
on the front of each shelf, that is to say, on the lower
board of each of the aforesaid shelves ; certain
letters, however, are excepted, namely A, H, K,
L, M, O, P, Q, which have no numbers affixed,
because all the volumes to which one of those letters
belongs are contained in the shelf to which that

letter is assigned.[1] Also all and singular the
volumes of the said library are fully marked on the
first leaf or outside on the table [2] or on both, with
certain numbered letters.   And in order that what
is in the library may be more quickly found, the
marking of the shelves of the said library, the
inscriptions in the books, and the references in the
register, in all points agree with each other.   Anno
Domini MCCCC.'

    ' The order in which the books of the monastery of
Tychefeld lie in the library of the said monastery.'
[1st Case, 1st shelf (A), *Theology*, 4 Bibles ; 2nd-6th
shelves (B), 18 Bibles with commentary ; 7th-8th
shelves (B), 7 comm. on Psalms.   2nd Case, 1st shelf
(C), 7 comm. on Bible ; 2nd (C), 3 comm. on Bible
and Isidorus ; 3rd (C), 6 theological volumes ; 4th
5th (D), 6 vols. of Gregory ; 6th (D), 2 theological
vols. ; 7th-8th (D), 4 Augustines.   3rd Case, 1st-
2nd shelves (E), 11 Lives of Saints and Sermons ;
3rd-4th (F), 11 vols. of *Canon Law ;* 5th-7th (G), 21
vols. of comm. on Canon Law ; 8th (H), 7 vols. of
Civil Law.   4th Case, 1st shelf (K), 29 vols. of
Medicine ; 2nd-3rd (L-M), *Arts*, 8 and 16 vols. of

    [1] That is, the shelves with the letters A, H, K, etc., have a
complete class of books in each, and in no case does that class
overflow into a second shelf, so there was no need of marking
these shelves with numbers as well as letters, in the way in
which the rest were marked.   Thus we should find ' B 1,' ' B 2,'
' B 3,' . . . ' B 7,' because B filled seven shelves ; but 'A'
only, because A filled *one* shelf alone.
    [2] That is, on the paper under horn sometimes fastened to
the outside of the binding of a MS., here apparently called
tabula.   It can hardly refer to the shelf on which the volume
rested, which is also *tabula.*

Grammar ; 4th-5th (N), 20 miscellaneous vols. ;
6th (O), 8 and 5 vols. of Logic and Philosophy ; 7th
(P), 13 vols. of English Law ; 8th (Q), 18 French
volumes. After these followed 102 liturgical
volumes.]

Titchfield Abbey was a Præmonstratensian house,
founded in the thirteenth century, and never
specially rich or prominent ; yet we find it with a
good library of sixty-eight books in theology, thirty-
nine in Canon and Civil Law, twenty-nine in
Medicine, thirty-seven in Arts, and in all three
hundred and twenty-six volumes, many containing
several treatises, so that the total number of works
was considerably over a thousand.

We will now consider a few of the famous libraries
existing in Great Britain and Ireland which contain
a large body of MSS., describing their gradual
building up, whether by donations or purchase of
manuscripts. Mr. Elton has already described (in
his volume on Book-Collectors in this series) some of
the chief private libraries of manuscripts ; the
present chapter will deal rather with the ultimate
resting-places of those private collections, in cases
where they have fortunately escaped dispersal by
sale or through neglect.

1. *The British Museum*

Among English-speaking peoples the library of
the British Museum stands without a rival, whether
we regard the size or the importance of its printed

and manuscript treasures. It is the National Library, the central collection of the literature of the British Empire, while it claims also to have the largest collection of the printed literature of every foreign country which exists outside that country. In the extent of its printed books it perhaps exceeds the National Library at Paris, and in the value of its MSS. ranks with the latter library and with the Vatican. It is the foremost library in the world.

Its foundation was comparatively late, but almost at once brought together four private collections of great extent, in 1753-7. First is the *Old Royal Library* of the Kings of England, which had grown to importance more by small and gradual accretions than by deliberate purchase on a large scale. Even Queen Elizabeth added little to it ; and not till, under James I., the Earl of Arundel's MSS. were added to it, can it be said to have received at any one time an important enlargement. Under White-lock's care it survived the Civil War ; but when Dr. Richard Bentley became keeper in 1694, it was still lodged in a mean room in St. James's Palace. Even when transferred to the British Museum in 1757, the MSS. only numbered 1800, but comprised such volumes as the Alexandrine Codex of the New Testament, and many royal possessions of special interest and value. The second collection was the celebrated *Cottonian* Library, the result of Sir Robert Bruce Cotton's energy. After his death in 1631, his son and grandson, Sir Thomas and Sir

John Cotton, augmented it, and in A.D. 1700 it was
vested by the latter for public purposes in the hands
of trustees. On Saturday, October 23, 1731, when
the library was at Ashburnham House in West-
minster, a terrible fire broke out, and damaged most
seriously over a hundred of the 958 MSS. of the
collection, and less seriously injured a hundred more.
Since then everything possible has been done to
restore the shrivelled and blackened leaves. The
fourteen original cases at Ashburnham House were
surmounted by busts of the twelve Cæsars, with
Cleopatra and Faustina, and the shelf-marks still
bear their name—the type of reference being MS.
Cotton *Caligula* D. vi., or the like. Chartularies of
English abbeys, English historical deeds, and a long
series of English State papers are among the chief
features of the library. Third in rank, but by far
the most numerous, is the *Harleian* Collection,
comprising nearly 8000 volumes, besides more than
14,000 charters and rolls. It was the result of the
efforts of Robert Harley, Earl of Oxford (*d.* 1724),
and Edward, his son, to amass volumes illustrating
English history ; but theology, classics and general
literature are almost equally well represented.
Parliament purchased it for £10,000, and in 1753 it
was transferred to the Museum. Smaller in size,
but more really the nucleus of the Museum, are the
library and museum of Sir Hans *Sloane*. The MSS.
number 4100, and are chiefly scientific, of the
sixteenth and seventeenth centuries ; but the

curiosities are the foundation of the Natural History Department, and the provident mind of Sir Hans Sloane had already sketched out a scheme by which his collections, valued by himself at £80,000, should be preserved for public use and entrusted to a body of trustees. After his death in 1752, the Act was passed (26 Geo. II. cap. 22, 1753) which established the British Museum, by purchasing Montagu House in Bloomsbury, Sir Hans Sloane's collections (for £20,000), and the Harleian Library, and for providing that the Cottonian Library should be transferred to the same place. The Old Royal Library was joined to these in 1757.

No large collection of MSS. was added to these four corner-stones of the National Library until 1807, when the *Lansdowne* collection (of State papers and other material for English history) was purchased, soon followed in 1813 by the legal MSS. of Francis Hargrave, and in 1818 by the classical and other MSS. of Dr. Charles Burney. The library collected by George III., which narrowly escaped a transfer to Russia, but ultimately became the property of the Museum in 1829, contained 440 manuscripts, chiefly bearing on the relations of England to France, and on the art of war.

With the purchase in 1831, from the Royal Society, of the MSS. of Thomas Howard, Earl of *Arundel* (which had been received by the Society in 1667, and were quite miscellaneous in character), and the bequest of the Hardwicke Papers in 922 volumes (1835), the second group of accessions was complete. Soon after this, immense progress was made in the printed department under Sir Antonio Panizzi, and the whole Museum became still more worthy of the nation. The Syriac collections, brought from the Nitrian desert in 1841-49, were the foundation of the Oriental MSS. In 1883 a precious collection of about 1000 Stowe MSS., forming part of the Ashburnham Library, was acquired ; and in it not only many volumes of English topography, genealogy, and political correspondence, but also Anglo-Saxon charters of great interest. Among the later accessions are the very choice bequests from Baron Ferdinand Rothschild (1898) and Mr. A. H. Huth (1911).

2. *Bodleian Library*

Next in importance among the libraries of the British Empire is the Bodleian Library at Oxford. Its founder, Sir Thomas Bodley, was a worthy of Devon, who had been actively employed by Queen Elizabeth as a diplomatist, and had returned tired of court life to the University, where long before he had been Fellow of Merton College. He found the ancient library of the University (which, after growing slowly with many vicissitudes from small beginnings, had suddenly been enriched in 1439-46 by a gift of 264 valuable MSS. from Humphrey, Duke of Gloucester) utterly destroyed by Edward VI.'s Commissioners, and the room built for its

H

reception (still called ' Duke Humphrey's library ')
swept clear even of the readers' desks. His determination to refound the library of the University
was actively carried out, and on November 8, 1602,
the new institution was formally opened with about
2000 volumes, of which 299 were MSS. Two
striking advantages were possessed by the Bodleian
almost from the first. Sir Thomas Bodley employed his great influence at court and with friends
to induce them to give help to his scheme, and
accordingly we find not only donations of money and
books from personal friends, but (for instance) 240
MSS. contributed by the Deans and Chapters of
Exeter and Windsor. Moreover, in 1610 he arranged with the Stationers' Company that they
should present his foundation with a copy of every
printed book published by a member of the Company ; and from that time to this the right to
every book published in the kingdom has been
almost continuously enjoyed. Before the Civil War
the chief accessions were the Barocci Greek MSS.
from the Earl of Pembroke (1629) ; Sir Kenelm
Digby's collection (1634) ; and Archbishop Laud's
large and valuable library of Oriental, classical, and
English volumes (1635-40), in all about 1300 MSS.
in more than twenty languages. At this time
Oxford was almost the only place where collectors
could place their treasures in safety ; and fortunately
so little did politics enter into the affairs of the
library, that both Fairfax and Cromwell not only

spared the building in the Civil War, but gave the MSS. still known by their names, and the former also the Dodsworth Collection. The other chief accessions of the seventeenth century were from Selden (1656) and the two Oriental scholars Pococke and Huntington, followed in 1713 by Archbishop Narcissus Marsh. In the first quarter of the eighteenth century no large donation was received, but at last in 1736 a series of large gifts began with Bishop Tanner's MSS., followed by the Clarendon State Papers in 1759, and the Carte Papers (relating to Irish and English history) ; while by Dr. Richard Rawlinson's will in 1755 upwards of 7000 MSS. came in, quite miscellaneous in subject, but including all Hearne's possessions, and teeming with the spoils of the manuscript sales of the previous half-century. No other large collection arrived until we reach the two great donations and the two great purchases of the nineteenth century—the Gough and Douce Libraries, and the Oppenheimer and Canonici Collections. The first (1809) was topographical, the next (1834) contributed nearly all the finest illuminations possessed by the Bodleian. The general collection of the Venetian Jesuit Canonici came in 1817, and the Hebrew MSS. and printed books of Oppenheimer in 1829. Several Oriental collections followed, Bruce's (Arabic and Ethiopic) in 1843, and Ouseley's (Persian) in 1844. By transference from the Ashmolean Museum, which was from the first rather a museum of natural history than a library, the

Bodleian received in 1860 the valuable Ashmole
and Anthony Wood Collections; the former full of
heraldic lore and genealogical matter, the latter of
Oxford antiquities. Sir Chandra Shum Shere presented 6330 Sanskrit MSS. in 1910, and in 1913 a
large Chinese library was received from Sir E.
Backhouse. Throughout its history the Bodleian
has derived much more from the good will of
benefactors than from any purchasing powers of its
own.

3. *Cambridge University Library*

The University Library at Cambridge is the most
ancient of all the more public collections in the
kingdom. There are books there which have been
continuously on the shelves since the first quarter of
the fifteenth century, having been presented in 1424.
A great landmark in the history of the library is
an inventory of the books (all at that time manuscript) taken in 1473, which exhibits the old arrangement as in a monastic library, with its five com-
partments devoted to Theology, three to Canon
Law, one each to Civil Law, Moral Philosophy,
Natural Philosophy, and Medicine, and one shared
by Logic and Grammar. In 1715, the library
received a very great augmentation in the library of
John Moore, Bishop of Ely, purchased and presented
by King George I. In more recent times, the
valuable library of Lord Acton (about 60,000
volumes) was presented in 1903 by Lord Morley, and

a large Chinese collection by Sir T. F. Wade in 1886. Its greatest treasure is the Codex Bezæ (see p. 83).

The Library of Trinity College, Dublin, had a curious origin, being a thank-offering on the part of the army which won the battle of Kinsale against Irish insurgents and their Spanish allies in 1601. But the foundation of its greatness was largely due to the fact that, after many vicissitudes both before and after its possessor's death in 1656, Archbishop Ussher's library, including nearly 700 valuable MSS., found its resting-place there. It possesses some of the grandest monuments of early Irish art, in the Book of Kells, the Book of Durrow, and similar volumes.

The colleges of Oxford and Cambridge (especially the older ones, and particularly Balliol, Merton, Christ Church, and Queen's at Oxford, and Trinity and Corpus Christi at Cambridge (the last-named possessing a splendid collection left to it by Archbishop Parker) contain MSS. of value, and most of the cathedrals have small collections ; while the Lambeth Library in London, the John Rylands in Manchester, and in Scotland the Advocates', would deserve special mention in a larger work than the present.

Among private libraries in the United Kingdom, one still overshadows the rest by its size, though much has now been dispersed by auction and private sale the Phillipps Collection at Thirlestane House,

Cheltenham.   It is hardly credible that the number
of MSS. was about 35,000.   Sir Thomas Phillipps of
Middlehill, in Worcestershire, amassed this number
by fairly sweeping the London market during the
period from 1823 to about 1870.   At first he was
careful to select important volumes, but in later
life he became less fastidious.   The only parallel to
Sir Thomas Phillipps' raids on the London market
is the curious condition attached to Dr. Mason's
bequest to Queen's College, Oxford, in 1841 : that
£30,000 should be spent on MSS. and rare printed
books within ten years.   The Phillipps MSS. chiefly
illustrate English history ; but more than 350 are
Greek, while Latin classics and the Fathers are well
represented ; and there is an immense body of documents relating to France, Italy, and Spain.

The number of papers, letters, and volumes of
public interest and value discovered by the Historical
Manuscripts Commission, and described in their
reports, has surprised persons who believed our
public libraries to contain almost all that was of
value in England ; and no mention of private
libraries can omit the name of the Duke of Devonshire (owner of the Benedictional of Æthelwold,
Bishop of Winchester in 963-984, written by Abbot
Godeman, and illuminated with scenes from the life
of Christ and figures of saints in such profusion and
artistic taste that it is probably the finest MS.
existing in private hands), or the treasures brought
together for sale by the late Mr. Bernard Quaritch,

or the astonishing MSS. owned by Mr. Yates Thompson in London and Mr. Dyson Perrins at Malvern.

The chief foreign libraries can only be summarily enumerated. The National Library at Paris has claims to be considered the finest in the world, if we put together its regal history, its present size, and the value of its contents. It has grown since the fourteenth century out of the collections of the French kings, and owes much to the pride with which not only France, but the ambassadors of France in foreign countries, have regarded it, as well as to the distinguished librarians who have fostered it, from De Thou and Colbert to M. Léopold Delisle. Vast accessions were obtained from the French religious houses suppressed at the Revolution, although it is said that at that time some 25,000 MSS. in provincial libraries were burnt.

Next ranks the Vatican at Rome, not for size, but for the intrinsic importance of its manuscript contents. The jealous care of the Popes from Nicholas V. in the fifteenth century, and their great opportunities for acquiring theological treasures, have been the sources of its security and increase. The Ambrosian Library at Milan, the Laurentian at Florence, with that of St. Mark at Venice, complete the list of important Italian collections. In Austria the great storehouse of MSS. is the Imperial Library at Vienna ; in the German Empire, the Libraries of Berlin and Munich ; in Holland, that of the Hague ;

in Belgium, the Royal Library of Brussels ; in
Russia, the Imperial Library of St. Petersburg ; and
in Spain, the Royal Library of Madrid and the
Escurial.

Even a cursory survey of these great libraries and
collections of MSS. suggests reflexions on principles
of ownership. How does a library acquire absolute
right over volumes which have once been in other
repositories ? When a man like Libri, the great
French book thief of the last century (who visited
officially certain provincial libraries and stole MSS.
therefrom, sometimes taking the trouble to substitute sham volumes bound like the originals), sells
his books to public libraries, have they full ownership at once in point of law ? Sir Robert Cotton
once lent a celebrated eighth century Psalter out of
his library (eventually the Cottonian Collection in
the British Museum), and passing from hand to hand
it was given at last by a M. de Ridder in 1718 to the
Utrecht Library, and is now known as the Utrecht
Psalter. Is there any possibility of its restitution ?
Henry Bradshaw recognized a valuable printed
Sarum Breviary of 1483 in the National Library at
Paris as stolen from the Cambridge University
Library since 1715, and purchased in 1825 by the
authorities of the Paris Library ; what rights exist
to reclaim the book ?

It would appear that the right to a book rests on
more than one consideration, certainly not simply

on the fact of justifiable acquisition, though after a considerable time that fact begins to have weight. Clearly when a lawful authority has authorized the dispersal of a collection, full ownership can be at once acquired. But failing this, the questions naturally asked are, Did the MS. come to its owners from a pure source, that is to say, from a seller of known good character, so that there is no suspicion of his being a conscious receiver of stolen goods ? and, Does the MS. now rest in a proper and accessible repository, so that no substantial injustice is done to the republic of letters ? If these two questions are affirmatively answered, probably no court of law would compel restitution. It has, however, been decided that in the case of parish registers, no bookseller can acquire or impart any rights of ownership, and that when found they are liable to be claimed by the authorities of the place to which they belong. But even in this case the lapse of time would have weight, if it exceeded say half a century. The facilities given by the British Government for the restoration of Libri volumes to France in 1883 form an interesting chapter in the history of international courtesy, but hardly touch the legal aspect of the question. The possibilities of photographic reproduction have much modified both the tension of feeling naturally caused in certain cases and the necessity of restitution.

CHAPTER VIII

FAMOUS MANUSCRIPTS

IN the present chapter, short descriptions will be given of a few of the best known manuscripts which have come down to us, arranged in order of date. Most of our examples are taken from manuscripts still preserved in the British Isles. Their vicissitudes and present state illustrate the dangers which have attended the precarious passage of these treasures across the ocean of time, and many bear traces of fights, of fire, and of shipwreck, in their voyage.

CIRCA B.C. 3000

Among the very oldest writing in the world, on stone, wood, papyrus, or parchment, is a monument, with an inscription in Egyptian Hieroglyphics (preserved in the Ashmolean Museum at Oxford), of which a representation is given opposite. It is the cornice over a false door of a tomb, the frame of the doorway being still in existence in the Gizeh Museum near Cairo, while a portion which bears an inscription was presented by Dr. Huntington to the University in 1683. At one side is a seated figure representing Shera, a priest of Send; at the other, another seated figure of a female. Between them is

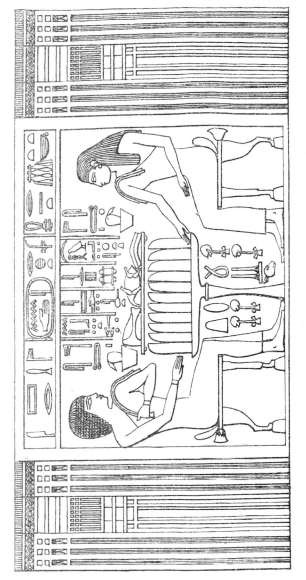

PLATE VII : SEND INSCRIPTION (B.C. 3000 ?)

a table, and on it and below it offerings made to Send.   This Send was a king of the second dynasty; and even if we allow his cult to have continued for centuries, the age of the stone would still have to be assigned to some such date as 3000 B.C. The astonishing thing is that, even in this remote antiquity, the inscription (the important part of which runs along the upper edge) exhibits, not only ideographic writing or only syllabic, but actually alphabetical!   The cartouche bearing the name of

the king is written alphabetically   thus :   (N D S)

= Send.   It adds to the interest of this venerable monument that Egyptian Hieroglyphics are in the direct line of the ancestry of our own alphabet (see p. 22).

(see p. 22)

B.C. 2500

The oldest piece of literary composition known, and the oldest book in existence, are to be found in the celebrated Papyrus Prisse, now in the Louvre at Paris.   It consists of eighteen pages in Egyptian Hieratic writing, ascribed to about the year B.C. 2500. But the treatise it contains claims to have been composed as long ago as about B.C. 3350.   Curiously enough, these first-fruits of the earliest ages are a treatise on how to behave wisely, the moralizings of an aged sage, a *laudator temporis acti*.   The early narratives embedded in the Book of Genesis may be

of equal antiquity, but materials for satisfactorily
dating them are at present wholly wanting.

Earliest Greek Writing
FOURTH CENTURY B.C.

The oldest known Greek writing is a papyrus
containing the *Persæ*, a play by Timotheus, assigned
to the second half of the fourth century B.C., and
now at Berlin. The next oldest is a woman's curse !
On a papyrus at Vienna, written in uncial characters,
and assigned to the early part of the third century
B.C., is found a prayer of one Artemisia, calling down
vengeance on the father of her dead child for
deserting her without supplying even the means
with which to bury the infant. This might almost
seem a chapter from a nineteenth century novel,
were it not that the ancient Greek attributed such
age-long consequences to neglect of burial, that
there is a stronger emotion in the scene than even
we could feel.

Earliest Latin Writing
A.D. 53

In contrast with the antiquity of Greek writing is
the fact that no Latin document is known which can
claim to be written before A.D. 50. The most
ordinary and prosaic incidents of life, described on
no more durable substance than wax, are the subject
of the Latin documents which have most successfully

defied the influence of time. Wax tablets containing
the record of sales and taxes, scratched with a stilus
in cursive letters, now in the National Museum at
Naples, and found at Pompeii in 1875, are clearly
dated from A.D. 53 onward, and at present take
precedence of all other known Latin documents
written by hand, except one papyrus which may be
of about A.D. 25.

BEFORE A.D. 79

Every reader of Pliny's *Epistles* remembers the
graphic description of the ' Last Days of Pompeii ; '
how his uncle, the elder Pliny, was in command of a
fleet at Misenum when his attention was called to
a column of thick smoke and vapour rising from
Vesuvius ; how he put to shore in order to observe
the phenomenon, and, after being driven from the
house where he was staying by the showers of ashes,
succumbed at last on the sea-shore, suffocated by
sulphurous fumes. The showers of ashes and the
streams of lava which overcame the elder Pliny
poured over the houses of Herculaneum and Pompeii,
filling the rooms, and by their heat reducing the
papyrus rolls of the private libraries there to black
and desiccated lumps. But what appeared to be
destruction was really the condition of safety ; for
after they were dug out in the second half of the
eighteenth century, it was found that, by the most
delicate treatment, many of them could be given
consistency enough to allow of unrolment, and finally
of decipherment. Fortunately, facsimiles were
carefully taken immediately after the unrolling, partly

under the Prince Regent's auspices in 1802-6 ; and
it is now found that the facsimiles are really of more
value than the originals, which, even when carefully
preserved, could hardly escape decay and disintegration.   Out of these rolls have come large fragments
of Philodemus, an Epicurean philosopher, in Greek,
and some Latin fragments of poems ; and it is quite
possible that in the future still more, and, we
may hope, more interesting, specimens of ancient
literature may be recovered.

Papyri from Egypt

Old burial grounds and temple rooms buried in
the sands of Egypt have given up astonishing
treasures since about 1850.   Orations by Hyperides,
the lost Ἀθηνῶν Πολιτεία of Aristotle, and the
mimes of Herodas may be mentioned, as well as
traditional sayings of Christ, and numberless fragments of classical Greek authors, but very little
Latin literature.   And among them are such delight-
ful pieces as the following schoolboy's letter in
Greek of the second or third century of our era :—
' Theon to his father Theon greeting.   It was a fine
thing of you not to take me with you to Alexandria.
Mother said to Archelaüs, " He quite upsets me.
Take him away." So send for me, I implore you.
If you don't, I won't eat, I won't drink.   There
now ! ' We may be pretty sure that after firing off
this blunderbuss at his father, the youthful Theon
sat down to a good dinner, and slept well.   The
father probably replied, after a chilling interval, that
he had better wait and see, and not upset his mother.

The Cottonian Genesis

In its original state this celebrated MS. contained
165 quarto leaves, bearing the text of Genesis in
Greek, written in uncials, with 250 miniature paintings.   It was probably written in the fourth century,
being the most ancient Greek Septuagint MS. on
parchment in existence, but is now, unfortunately, a
mass of blackened fragments, some better preserved
than others, having been the chief victim in that
terrible fire, so often referred to in this volume,
which half ruined the Cottonian Collection in 1731.
We have, however, collations of the text made before
the fire, so that the loss, so far as the text is con-
cerned, is not wholly irreparable ; but the very size
of the letters was altered by the heat, and the
paintings practically destroyed.

The Codex Sinaiticus

The story of the discovery of this famous manuscript of the Bible in Greek, the oldest existing of all
the New Testament codexes, and in several points
the most interesting, reads like a romance.   Constantine Tischendorf, the well-known editor of the
Greek Testament, started on his first *mission littéraire*
in April 1844, and in the next month found himself
at the Convent of St. Catherine, at the foot of Mount
Sinai.   There, in the middle of the hall, as he crossed
it, he saw a basket full of old parchment leaves on
their way to the burning, and was told that two

baskets had already gone ! Looking at the leaves
more closely, he perceived that they were parts of
the Old Testament in Greek, written in an extremely
old handwriting. He was allowed to take away
forty-three leaves ; but the interest of the monks
was aroused, and they both stopped the burning and
also refused to part with any more of the precious
fragments. Tischendorf departed, deposited the
forty-three leaves in the Leipzig Library, and edited
them under the title of the Codex Friderico-
Augustanus, in compliment to the King of Saxony,
in 1846. But he wisely kept the secret of their
provenance, and no one followed in his track until
he himself went on a second quest to the monastery
in 1853. In that year he could find no traces
whatever of the remains of the MS. except a few
fragments of Genesis, and returned unsuccessful and
disheartened. At last, he once more took a journey
to the monastery, under the patronage of the
Russian Emperor, who was popular throughout the
East as the protector of the Oriental Churches.
Nothing could he find, however ; and he had ordered
his Bedouins to get ready for departure, when,
happening to have taken a walk with the steward of
the house, and to be invited into his room, in the
course of conversation the steward said : ' I, too,
have read a Septuagint,' and produced out of a
wrapper of red cloth ' a bulky kind of volume,'
which turned out to be the whole of the New Testament, with the Greek text of the Epistle of Barnabas,

much of which was hitherto unknown, and the greater part of the Old Testament, all parts of the very MS. which had so long been sought! In a careless tone Tischendorf asked if he might have it in his room for further inspection, and that night (February 4-5, 1859) it 'seemed impiety to sleep.' By the next morning the Epistle of Barnabas was copied out, and a course of action was settled. Might he carry the volume to Cairo to transcribe? Yes, if the Prior's leave were obtained; but unluckily the Prior had already started to Cairo on his way to Constantinople. By the activity of Tischendorf he was caught up at Cairo, gave the requisite permission, and a Bedouin was sent to the convent, and returned with the book in nine days. On the 24th of February, Tischendorf began to transcribe it; and when it was done, conceived the happy idea of asking for the volume as a gift to the Emperor of Russia. Probably this was the only possible plea which would have gained the main object in view, and even as it was there was great delay; but at last, on the 28th of September, the gift was formally made, and the MS. soon after deposited at Petrograd, where it perhaps now lies. The age of this MS. (known as א) is supposed to be not later than A.D. 400, and has been the subject of dispute, partly in consequence of the curious statement of Simonides in 1862, that he had himself written it on Mount Athos in 1839-40 (see p. 142). For other great Biblical MSS. see p. 82.

The Book of Kells

The Book of Kells, the chief treasure of Trinity College, Dublin, is so called from having been long preserved at the Monastery of Kells, founded by Columba himself. Stolen from thence, it eventually passed into Archbishop Ussher's hands, and, with other parts of his library, to Dublin. The volume contains the Four Gospels in Latin, ornamented with extraordinary freedom, elaboration, and beauty. Written apparently in the seventh century, it exhibits, both in form and colour, all the signs of the full development and maturity of the Irish style, and must of necessity have been preceded by several generations of artistic workers, who founded and improved this particular school of art. The following words of Professor Westwood, who first drew attention to the peculiar excellences of the volume, will justify the terms made use of above :—

' This copy of the Gospels, traditionally asserted to have belonged to Columba, is unquestionably the most elaborately executed MS. of early art now in existence, far excelling, in the gigantic size of the letters in the frontispieces of the Gospel, the excessive minuteness of the ornamental details, the number of its decorations, the fineness of the writing, and the endless variety of initial capital letters with which every page is ornamented, the famous Gospels of Lindisfarne in the Cottonian Library. But this MS. is still more valuable on account of the various pictorial representations of different scenes in the life of our Saviour, delineated in a style totally unlike that of every other school.' The frontispiece will give some idea of the regularity and beauty of the ornamentation, and of the minuteness and profusion of it, though not of the striking harmonies of colour.

The next MS. which would naturally be mentioned is the Lindisfarne Gospels, in the British Museum, of the seventh century ; but as being already described in this series of books (see Mr. Elton's *The Great Book-Collectors*, p. 18), it is here omitted, so far as relates to its general history and description. But the Lindisfarne Gospels exhibit another point of great interest not there recorded. Each Gospel is preceded by a list, in the order of the Gospel itself, of saints' days, feasts, vigils, etc., on which passages from that Gospel were read ; that is to say, the first days recorded are those on which passages from the first chapter were read, and so on. In 1891 a Benedictine monk observed that the lists clearly proved that the liturgy thus summarized was that of Naples, and was of extreme interest, being more than two centuries older than the oldest known Neapolitan calendar. But how was it possible for an early calendar of Naples to appear in a Gospel book written at Lindisfarne or Holy Island, off the Northumbrian coast, in the seventh century ? The answer is supplied by Bede, who, in describing the early work of Theodore of Tarsus, Archbishop of Canterbury, after his arrival in England in 668, says that in his peregrination of England he was accompanied by one Adrian, formerly abbot of a monastery near Naples. At Lindisfarne the archbishop was to consecrate St. Aidan's new cathedral, and there can be no reasonable doubt that the abbot brought with him some volumes from his own abbey, and that the monks of Holy Island took the opportunity of transcribing for their own use this volume. Curiously enough, another less famous MS., also in the British Museum (in the Old Royal Collection), is found to have the same calendar prefixed, and doubtless was written at the same place and time. Directly, the volumes lead us back to the services of Naples in the first half of the seventh century, that is to say, of the time of St. Gregory ; indirectly, they lead to something still more striking.   Naples is not far from Rome ; and when it is remembered that no extant MSS. carry us beyond the seventh century in the quest of ancient Roman service books, the real value of these two MSS. becomes clear.   They present to us one of the nearest attainable clues to the most ancient liturgical ceremonies of Rome itself.

Alcuin's Bible

The connexion of Alcuin of York with the literary reforms of Charles the Great has been already referred to (see p. 29).   It was natural that the head of the school of Tours should show gratitude to his patron on so great an occasion as the coronation of

Charles the Great as Emperor of Rome on Christmas Day in A.D. 800 ; and from contemporary sources we know that this gratitude took the form of a Latin Bible written under the immediate superintendence of Alcuin, and with a text emended by himself.

There is still in existence a Latin Bible directly ascribed to Alcuin himself, a volume bought in 1836 by the British Museum, which sufficiently answers to everything which we know of the circumstances of the gift, and certainly represents Alcuin's revision of the Vulgate text. At the end are certain verses in which the writer's name is given as Alcuinus and Albinus (a not infrequent variety of the former name). It is a splendid volume, both in size and from the four full-page illuminations which, with other smaller paintings, adorn the text. It is known, however, that similar verses are found in another Latin Bible now at Rome, so that the claim of this volume to be the actual gift of the great English scholar and teacher to the Emperor who honoured him is not incontestable, and the date is asserted to be more probably forty years later than 800.

The Old English Chronicle

The chronological Annals of England, known familiarly as the Anglo-Saxon Chronicle, are said to be the finest existing record, having regard to its antiquity and detail, of the early history of any European nation. They begin, after a brief preface,

with Julius Cæsar's landing in England, B.C. 65 ; and
though at first affording notices of general history,
soon settles down to a history of Britain alone. The
MSS. we possess of it are extremely interesting in
their differences, for almost every one contributes
local colouring and local history to the common
stock, and each carries the chronicle proper down to
a different date. Six complete MSS. still exist :
one in the splendid library bequeathed by Archbishop Parker to Corpus Christi Library at Cambridge, which was written in 891 and continued to
1070, and which, having been first at Winchester,
was transferred before it was finally completed to
Christ Church, Canterbury ; a second, written in
one hand, and ending with A.D. 977, now in the
British Museum (Cotton *Tiberius*, A. vi.), but formerly also at Canterbury, and noticeable for the
incorporation (as is the case also with the next two
MSS.) of a Mercian chronicle for the years 902-924 ;
a third, an Abingdon chronicle, written in one hand
to 1046, and continued to 1066, and now in the
British Museum (Cotton *Tiberius*, B. i.) ; a fourth
from Worcester, embodying some Northumbrian
annals, written in 1016, with additions to 1079, now
also in the National Library (Cotton *Tiberius*, B. iv.) ;
a fifth, given by Archbishop Laud to the Bodleian
(Laud *Misc.* 636), abounding in Peterborough
history, and though written in A.D. 1122, continued in
Peterborough Abbey to 1154, which is three-
quarters of a century beyond any other ; and

lastly, a Canterbury MS. of the twelfth century, curious for being bilingual, in Saxon and Latin, and now in the Museum (Cotton *Domitian*, A. viii.). A seventh was burnt, with the exception of three leaves, in the fatal fire of 1731 (Cotton *Otho*, B. xi.), but is known from previous editions, and ended in A.D. 1001 ; and a single leaf of an eighth is known in yet another Cotton MS. (*Domitian*, A. ix.). This wealth of material gives every facility for a thorough knowledge of the Chronicle, difficult as it is to determine the method and date of its original formation. It is quite possible that Alfred himself ordered its compilation, and at any rate it was formed after Bede's death in 735, and before 895, when Asser, the biographer of Alfred, quotes it.

Beowulf

The great fire of 1731, which caused such irreparable damage to the Cottonian Library, mutilated and nearly deprived us for ever of the earliest English epic, and, with the possible exception of Widsith, of the earliest known English poem. This is known by the name of Beowulf, the hero whose combats with the fiend Grendel and with a dragon, and death from his wounds, form the subject of the book. The scene professes to be laid in Denmark, and most German scholars attribute its formation (out of older materials) to about the year 600 ; but the late Professor Earle believed that the object of the book was to instruct the English folk

of the time of Offa, King of Mercia, in the true
education and feelings of a prince.   It is supposed,
therefore, by him to have been written in the eighth
century, on English soil, though it has survived to
our time only in a single MS. of about the date 1000,
of which the first notice of any kind is not earlier
than A.D. 1705, and the first printed edition that of
Thorkelin in 1815.   The language is Anglo-Saxon.

Caedmon

The earliest personal name in the history of English literature is that of Caedmon, the cow-herd of
Whitby, about the middle of the seventh century.
Bede, who had good opportunities for knowing the
facts about him, tells us how, when each person after
supper had to sing a song to his harp, and the turn
came to Caedmon, he would slink out, ashamed and
stupid, rather than attempt to sing.   But in a dream
a voice said to him, ' Caedmon, sing, sing something
to me ' ; and when he pleaded ignorance and
incapacity, and inquired what he should sing,
' Sing,' said the voice, ' the beginning of created
things.'   Then Caedmon broke out into impromptu
song ; and when the matter came to the ears of
Hilda, the foundress and first Abbess of Whitby, she
caused him to be educated, and exercise his gift of
song as a monk.   A few of his actual words seem to
be preserved to us by Bede ; but one MS., preserved
in the Bodleian, has long been believed to contain,
in a modified form, some part of the poems of
Caedmon.   The name of the poet does not occur,

Noe g\u0180uſme. ⁊þa hine nengþro heht hynoe þam hal
gan. hſbþon cyninge ongan. oþoꝛtlice· ꝥ hof þyꝛean·
micle mtһe cuʞte· magum ꞃægde· ꝥ þæꞃ þnſulic þing·
þꞃboum coꝛſꝼano· neðe þꞃte· hie nepohꞇon þæꞃ· ge
ꞃ\u0101h þa ymb þinꞇua þonn· þꞃn ſæꞃꞇ miꞇoð· gſbþon
huꞃa mæꞃꞇ· g\u0100no hlꞃꝼg\u0101n· innon ꞇuꞇun· ꞇonðan
ume· g\u01ffþꞃꞇoo p\u01ff ꝼloðe· þꞃn noꞃ\u00feꞇ· þꞃ ꞃelꞇꞇun·
ꝼ iꞃ ꞃynoꞃuᵹ cynn· Symle bꞃ\u01ff þꞃ h\u0100nona· þehir hꞃꞇꞃh
þꞃꞇꞃ· ꝛꝼ\u0101unꞇꞃ ꞃæ ꞃꞇꞃ\u0101unaꞃ· ꞃꝛꞇ\u01ffoꞃ b\u0100nꞇꞃ\u01ff·

PLATE VIII: CAEDMON (c. 1000, English).

but the contents agree fairly closely with what we know from Bede were the subjects of our first English poet's songs. These are, of course, all religious, consisting of metrical paraphrases of Genesis, Exodus, and parts of Daniel, with descriptions of scenes in Christ's life and of the day of judgment. Modern critics are disposed to deny any connexion between these West Saxon poems and the Northumbrian songs of Caedmon, but it is still at least probable that this MS., written like that of Beowulf about 1000, contains a substratum and, as the writer in the *Dictionary of National Biography* is willing to admit, some whole passages from the poet himself. Not the least interesting feature of the MS. is the drawings, chiefly in outline, with slight colouring, with which it abounds. They are of genuine Old English character, and are valuable, not for their fidelity to the subject to be elucidated, but for the evidences they afford of contemporary English life. Thus, when the ark is to be delineated, the artist racks his brain to think of the largest ship which he has ever seen, and presents us (see the illustration opposite) with a picture of a Scandinavian war galley, with carved figurehead, the side paddle used for steering, and many of the details of the Viking ship discovered in Norway some years ago. On the deck of this he places a large box to contain the animals. So, too, the architectural details of some buildings here drawn are of value for determining the style of church building of that period.

St. Margaret's Gospel-Book

The figure of St. Margaret, Queen of Scotland, is perhaps the most striking in the early history of that kingdom. Having regard to the rough times of the eleventh century, and her great personal influence, we may say that she did more to refine and civilize a nation than any mediæval queen before or after her. No wonder that the Scotch cherish her memory with especial reverence, and that her oratory in Edinburgh Castle is to them one of the most venerated relics of the past. Grand-daughter of Edmund Ironside, sister of Edgar the Atheling, and mother of the wife of Henry I., she is in the direct line by which our present king traces his descent from the English kings before the Conquest. Margaret fled before the Conqueror to Scotland, and sought refuge in the court of Malcolm Canmore, King of Scotland, who, about A.D. 1070, married her. For details of her character and life from this period till her death in 1093, no better account can be wished than her Life written by one who knew her intimately, printed in the Bollandist Acta Sanctorum and elsewhere, and issued in English by Father William Forbes-Leith (2nd ed., London 1889). The discovery of her most treasured volume, which she must often have used within the splendid choir of Dunfermline Abbey, where she was married, has preserved, it may be hoped, to all time a volume, small indeed in size, but of the deepest interest alike to the antiquary, the Church historian, and the liturgiologist.

In 1887 a little octavo volume in worn brown binding stood on the shelves of a small parish library in Suffolk, but was turned out and offered at the end of a sale at Sotheby's, presumably as being unreadable to country folk, and capable of being turned into hard cash wherewith a few works of fiction might be purchased. The contempt for it thus displayed was apparently shared by the cataloguer, who described it as Latin Gospels of the Fourteenth Century, with Illuminations. For the sum of £6 it passed into the Bodleian Library, and came to be catalogued as an ordinary accession. It was noticed that the writing was of the eleventh century, and that the illuminations were valuable specimens of old English work of the same century, comprising figures of the four evangelists of the Byzantine type, which was common in the west of Europe ; the drapery, however, colouring and accessories were purely English. The book itself was seen to be not the complete Gospels, but such portions as were used in the service of the Mass at different times of the year. Further, it was observed that a poem in Latin hexameters had been written, apparently before the end of the same century, on a fly-leaf of the volume, which began by thanking Christ for ' displaying miracles to us in our own days,' and went on to describe how this very volume had been carried in the folds of a priest's robe to a trysting-place, in order that a binding oath might be taken on it ; but that unfortunately it had been dropped, without the priest observing it, into a stream, and given up for lost. But a soldier of the party was sent back, who discovered it, plunged head first into the river, and brought it up. To everyone's intense surprise, the beautiful volume was entirely uninjured, ' except two leaves, which you see at each end, in which a slight contraction appears from the effect of the water, which testify the work of Christ in protecting the sacred volume. That this work might appear to us still more miraculous, the wave washed from the middle of the book a leaf of silk. May the King and pious Queen be saved for ever, whose book was but now saved from the waves ! ' The silk, was, no doubt, pieces placed loosely in the book to preserve the illuminations from contact with the page opposite ; and, sure enough, a leaf at each end of the book showed unmistakable crinkling from immersion in water. But who were the King and Queen ? By a curious accident connected with the name of Margaret, a lady to whom this story was told remembered a similar incident in Forbes-Leith's edition of the *Life of St. Margaret*, and the mystery was solved. There in the Life is a passage in prose, beginning : ' She had a book of the Gospels beautifully adorned with gold and precious stones, and ornamented with the figures of the four evangelists, painted and gilt. . . . She had always felt a particular attachment for this book,

more so than for any of the others which she usually
read.' Then follows a story almost identical with
the one given above, with some variant but not
discrepant details. It, too, mentions the pieces of
silk and the contraction on certain leaves, and adds
that it was found lying *open* at the bottom of the
river. If anything could add to the interest of the
volume, it is that in the same Life we read of the
King, that 'although he could not read, he would
turn over and examine books which the Queen used
either for her devotions or her study ; and whenever
he heard her express especial liking for a particular
book, he also would look at it with special interest,
kissing it, and often taking it into his hands.'

A Royal Psalter

The fortunes of MSS. are well illustrated by a
MS. now in Exeter College Library at Oxford. It
is a Latin Psalter, followed, as usual, by canticles, a
litany and prayers, beautifully illuminated in English style, and from the joint occurrence of the Royal
arms and those of Bohun, and the occurrence of the
name Humphrey in a collect, probably written and
painted for Humphrey de Bohun, Earl of Hereford
(*d.* 1361), grandson of Edward I., whose grandniece
was married to Henry IV. in 1380. Through her it
passed into the Royal Library ; but seems specially
to have belonged to the Queens, for both Elizabeth
of York and Katherine of Arragon have written
their names. In the calendar are obits of the Royal

family up to the time of Henry VIII., and no doubt it passed to Elizabeth. She seems to have parted with it to Sir William Petre, the re-founder of Exeter College, to which he presented it. Thus it happens that the successive possession of the Tudor sovereigns, and the original authority for the exact date of the birth of the founder of the Tudor dynasty (Jan. 28, ' Hic natus est rex Henricus vij^{us},' 145$\frac{5}{6}$), has dropped into a quiet college library.

The foregoing are a selection, as numerous as the scale of the present work would allow, of some well-known MSS. of great libraries ; but even though the volumes described are nearly all within the British Isles, the list is very far from exhausted. No place has been found for the Verona Codex of Sulpicius Severus, dated A.D. 517, the earliest dated vellum MS. ; for the splendid Hiberno-Saxon MSS. other than the Book of Kells and the Lindisfarne Gospels, such as the Chad Gospels at Lichfield, the Gospels of M'Durnan at Lambeth, and several more ; for the Benedictional of St. Ethelwold (see p. 102) ; for an original of Magna Charta in the British Museum ; for the Paston Letters, a unique example of English domestic correspondence from 1422 to 1509 ; or for the Syriac version of Genesis and Exodus, dated A.D. 464, and believed to be the earliest dated MS. extant of any entire book of the Scriptures ; or for the treasures of foreign libraries. But, indeed to give an account of such MSS. as suggest themselves as famous, would require a volume of itself, and turn a manual like the present into a catalogue.

CHAPTER IX

LITERARY FORGERIES

FORGERIES occupy no inconsiderable part of literary history, and it is even true that Palæography, the study of ancient writing, began in the endeavour to supply tests by which genuine deeds of a legal kind could be established, and forgeries detected. In the great Benedictine work by Mabillon, *De Re Diplomatica* (1681, etc.), a vast treatise, written with this particular object, the whole of Book iv., or nearly one-sixth of the entire work, is taken up with a list of 163 palaces belonging to the kings of France. This would seem irrelevant, until we understand that one of the greatest difficulties which a forger of some deed of gift would encounter, would be to know where the king was at any particular date which he might select for his spurious work. This list, therefore, supplies an invaluable means of detecting any mistake in the place where the deed is supposed to have been executed, the name of which would almost certainly occur in a genuine deed, and therefore must be somehow supplied by the forger. But the forgeries of legal deeds were, as a rule, tracked out by the sagacity of lawyers ; and the really gigantic frauds of literature have been perpetrated in the fields of theology or of history.

Before we give illustrations of some famous literary forgeries, it will be well if we try to enter into the forger's mind, for it must be admitted that the subject introduces us to what may be called a high and refined order of crime. Forgery of a literary document, to be successful, requires an intellect of no ordinary acuteness. Not only has a style to be imitated, but numberless inter-dependent facts of a particular time and place have to be profoundly studied. Usually facts have to be added which are not to be found in existing authorities, to give an air of original knowledge, and these guesses must be capable of satisfying the ever-increasing knowledge and the soundest methods of criticism of the age. Undesigned coincidences are among the subtlest solvents of a forgery, and proofs of a genuine record. Old paper with its appropriate watermarks, or parchment carefully stained, has to be provided and duly discoloured : the ink must be of the right tint and appearance, and the writing, not slowly and falteringly traced, but of a firm, boldly drawn kind. The forger, in fact, has to be armed at every point, and the cost of the armour is fortunately, in many cases, prohibitive. But when once obtained, as in the case of Constantine Simonides, the fraud seems to have a veritable fascination for acute and unprincipled adventurers. Again, forgery, really to deserve the name, must be made with intent to

deceive, whether that deception be for purely
humorous purposes or for sordid gain.   For we may
remember the example of Thucydides, who deliberately puts rhetorical speeches, which belong both in
point of thought and expression to his own time, in
the mouths of his characters, yet neither deceived
nor intended to deceive his Athenian readers.   This
case, which, of course, is not one of forgery, yet
shows how carefully its characteristics have to be
defined.   But even when the aim is reprehensible,
it is not enough to put down all forgeries under one
class—it is essential to take into consideration both
the character of the man and the moral standard of
his time.   There is a wide difference between Chatterton, whose boyish mind was entranced by the old
papers he found in the muniment room of St. Mary
Redcliffe at Bristol, seeing in them a means of building up a reputation, while himself far too young to
be treated as a precocious man of the world ; and
such machinators as Vrain-Lucas or Shapira, whose
sole thought was the money to be gained by their
scheming.   Between them may rank the men who,
conscious of great powers both of mind and hand,
and under considerable temptation, deliberately set
themselves to forge and foist on the world some of
the lost treatises of antiquity, either to support
preconceived theories of their own, or enjoying the
excitement and the uncertainty, the sense of
superiority in the hour of success, and the boldness
of their bid for that success.

K

The interest of forgeries for the student of literature lies in the method of detection. The same tests which expose the spurious work establish tenfold the character of what remains. It is the clear cut which they enable us to make between truth and seeming truth which shows that these tests are of real value.

1. *The Letters of Phalaris*

Phalaris was ' tyrant ' or petty king of Agrigentum in Sicily in the sixth century B.C., and for a thousand years no writings of his were known. At last Stobæus, in the fifth century A.D., quoted from his letters, and the existing Epistles were generally received as genuine. In fact, in the controversy which arose in the latter part of the seventeenth century on the comparative merits of ancient and modern literature, Sir William Temple went so far as to write (in 1680), ' I think the Epistles of *Phalaris* to have more Race, more Spirit, more Force of Wit and Genius, than any others I have ever seen. . . . I think he must have little Skill in Painting, that cannot find out this to be an Original,' with much to the same effect. This language stimulated the Scholars of Christ Church at Oxford, who were in the habit of producing a classical book once a year, to issue an edition of the Epistles, which was entrusted to the Hon. Robert Boyle, and appeared in 1695. It would probably have excited little attention, but that the one great critic which England

had produced, Dr. Richard Bentley, inserted in the
second edition of his friend William Wotton's *Reflections upon Ancient and Modern Learning* (1697), a
Dissertation upon the Epistles of Phalaris, which
appeared, not only to contemporary scholars, but to
all succeeding critics, a very miracle of learning,
logic, humour and ingenuity ; in fact, in the opinion
of no mean scholar of the nineteenth century, ' he
so absolutely settled the question, that to a very dolt
the maintenance of the genuineness of the Epistles
of Phalaris must seem absurd.' The triumph was
not immediate, for an attempted answer to it was
published by Boyle in 1698, which drew from
Bentley in the following year the second and
complete edition of his *Dissertation*. The celebrated
Boyle and Bentley controversy went on for some
years, but nothing could shake the greatness of the
Cambridge *Dissertation*, and it is still acknowledged
as the greatest product of English scholarship in the
eighteenth century.

Bentley's method was not to examine the MSS.
for signs of falsity, for no MSS. of the date of the
forger are extant, much less the forger's autograph,
but simply to rely on the internal evidence of the
letters themselves. Before his dissecting-knife they
fell to pieces. Towns were found to be mentioned
which were founded after Phalaris. The Messenians
and Zancleans are both named, though Zancle was
only the old name of Messene, the two towns being
one and the same ; Phalaris is angry with a poet

who wrote tragedies against him, though both the
name and thing were unknown till later ; the letters
are in an Attic dialect instead of the Doric of Sicily,
and not even in the Attic of Phalaris' time, but in
New Attic. So, too, the coins mentioned are wrong,
and wrong just as a forger would go astray ; for
when he speaks of talents, the computation shows
that he is thinking of *Attic* talents, each of which
was worth 2,000 Sicilian talents. Finally, Bentley
shows that words were used in a sense first given
them by Plato, and points out numerous incon-
sistencies in the matter itself. But these points
are elucidated with so much solid first-hand learning,
with such freshness, and in so humorous and per-
suasive a style, that in spite of the immense strides
we have since taken in these very departments of
knowledge, the *Dissertation* is still thoroughly instructive as well as entertaining reading.

2. *The False Decretals*

The early history of Church Law, like the history
of the Canon of the New Testament, abounds with
apocryphal and spurious works, though it is often
difficult to say with what amount of deliberate desire
to mislead they were fabricated. The first two
documents of Canon or Church Law are spurious,
the Apostolic Constitutions and the Apostolic
Canons, neither having any connexion with the
apostles themselves. They are, however, venerable
documents, and throw a clear light on the history of

the time when they were fabricated. Several genuine collections of Canons of ecclesiastical councils were made in succeeding centuries ; and among them the *Hispana* (sc. collectio), representing chiefly Spanish Canon Law, attained celebrity. At last, in the ninth century, one Isidorus Mercator (often confused with the greater Isidor, Bishop of Seville) edited the *Hispana*, but foisted into it no less than ninety-five fictitious Decretals (or authoritative letters from popes to bishops on points in dispute), the earliest professing to be dated A.D. 101 ! They were recognized as genuine by Pope Nicholas I. in A.D. 865, who did not scruple to assure Hincmar, against whom they were used, that the originals had lain for centuries in the Roman archives. They were, in fact, accepted everywhere until the fifteenth century, when, under the criticism of Valla Erasmus and others, they dissolved away. The extent to which the claims of the Papacy were affected by these convenient forgeries is a keenly-debated point ; but while it is clear, on the one hand, that the intention of the False Decretals was mainly to protect the bishops from the interference of both laymen and councils, yet the policy they professed to initiate, of an appeal to the pope in all greater causes, did certainly aid the popes in their later struggles for temporal power ; and the *Decretum* of Gratian (in the eleventh century), which is at the base of the system of Canon Law, certainly received and incorporated these forged documents.

3. *Ingulphus*

Among the monastic chronicles of England, the most considerable forgery is that of the Latin *History of the Abbey of Croyland*, attributed to Ingulphus, an abbot of that monastery, who died in 1109. The historian Ordericus Vitalis went to Croyland within a few weeks of Ingulphus' death, collected all the information he could get on the spot, gives us a considerable and authentic account of him, and says no word of his having written a detailed history of the abbey. When the narrative is looked into, the usual signs of imposture appear. The original charters of the house, which are quoted in full, abound with errors—bishops attest deeds before their appointment or after their death, names of places are spelt before the Conquest as they were spelt in the fifteenth century, feudal words occur too early, lands are granted (in A.D. 1013) for one hundred years at a nominal rent when neither kind of condition was in use in England before the Conquest, and the like. So, too, in the narrative itself, Ingulphus describes his education at Oxford, where he studied Cicero and Aristotle, at a time when Aristotle was in no part of Christendom studied at all; and admits numerous anachronisms both of language and fact. The curious thing is that four out of five known MSS. of the work have disappeared since A.D. 1600. One ' very ancient ' one, described as the autograph of Ingulphus, used to be kept at Croyland under lock and key, but disappeared in the middle of the seventeenth century ; a Cotton MS. which Selden used was burnt in the great fire of 1731 (see p. 95) ; Marsham's codex cannot be traced after about 1690, and Sir Henry Savile's is utterly lost. All that remains is an Arundel MS. in the British Museum, written in the sixteenth century ! This circumstance, and the solid substratum of fact which the History undoubtedly displays (though apparently only adapted from Ordericus Vitalis and others), have induced several modern critics to uphold this suspicious record, and to ascribe its errors to ignorant embellishers But the fact remains that no statement in the entire History can be accepted without corroboration, and that every note of imposture may be found in its pages.

4. *Chatterton*

Thomas Chatterton, the boy-poet, was born in poor circumstances in the parish of St. Mary Redcliffe at Bristol. In early years he had access, not only to the church itself, where heraldry and monumental effigies caught the eye at every turn, but also to the muniment room, where ' Canynge's Coffer,' a massive chest, once secured by six keys, but then forced and lying open, supplied numerous opportunities of studying the style and characters of ancient writing. These surroundings and the few books to which he had access predisposed a mind of great power and activity to the study of old English (for the boy never learnt Latin), and he soon

compiled a double glossary, of old words with their
modern meanings, and of current words with their
ancient equivalents. The first use he made of his
special knowledge and powers was to produce, in
1764, his twelfth year, a poem entitled 'Elinoure
and Juga.' In 1765 he had conceived the idea of
making Thomas Rowley, a supposed monk, the
fictitious author of several poems. Three years
after, Bristol Bridge was reopened with some cere-
mony, and the city was startled by an elaborate
narrative in a newspaper of the first passage of the
Mayor over the bridge in 1248. The interest this
excited stimulated Chatterton to produce in the
same year the best of his poems, the tragical inter-
lude of Ælla. Next we find the youth bold enough
to write to Horace Walpole, enclosing some old
English poems ; but the great man, after a short
time of uncertainty, showed his applicant the cold
shoulder, and returned the poems. The last period of
Chatterton's short and clouded life was spent in London, where, after some bold bids for fame, and chilling
failures, he put an end to his life on August 25, 1770.

In Chatterton's forgeries we find the least occasion
that can be imagined for wholesale condemnation,
and the greatest for pity and indulgence. To his
family and even to his friends he confessed, under
very little pressure, the simple truth, and the
greatest harm he did was to himself. Critics soon
saw that the language of the Rowley poems was a
mixture of the forms and vocabulary of all past

time, and that the matter teemed, as was inevitable,
with anachronisms and impossibilities. Poems in
the author's own name would have secured attention
and brought him reputation, so that meanness at
least was wanting to his deceit. And we cannot
but wonder what future would have been in store,
under happier conditions, for one of whom Walpole
could say that he knew of no one with so masterly
a genius, and who even drew from Johnson the
testimony that he was the most extraordinary
young man that had encountered his knowledge.

5. *The Ireland Forgeries*

The temporary success of what are known as the
Ireland forgeries, so lately as the close of the
eighteenth century, can only make us wonder at the
invincible credulity of mankind. William Henry
Ireland, born in 1777, was the son of a small pub-
lisher and bookseller who was enthusiastic about
Shakespeare and Shakespeariana. The temptation
to the son to play upon his father's weakness was too
strong to be resisted, and as early as 1794 the latter
was shown a lease purporting to be signed by
Shakespeare. The success of this practical joke led
to further results. Shakespeare's love-letters, one
enclosing a lock of his hair, and countless similar
relics, were produced, and a statement that they were
given by the poet to William Henrye Irelaunde [1] in
gratitude for a rescue from drowning. The father,

[1] *Two* ordinary Christian names hardly occur before 1700.

who was quite innocently duped, published these,
and many persons accepted them as genuine. At
last, as might have been foreseen, a complete play
was discovered, with the title 'Vortigern,' and
Sheridan actually produced it on April 2nd (it
should have been the 1st !), 1796, at Drury Lane
Theatre. The preparation for this was the crowning
point of Ireland's triumph ; for as soon as the play
was printed and studied, both the language and
sentiments betrayed the fraud. This prevented the
appearance of Henry II., another play which had
already been written ; and in the same year came a
crushing exposure from the pen of Edmund Malone,
the Shakespearian commentator, and also both
immediately and in 1805 a confession by Ireland
himself, in which he displays a certain amount of
satisfied vanity at the success he attained.

The extraordinary scantiness of our knowledge of
Shakespeare's personal life, and of the authority
and relationship of the Folio and Quarto editions of
his plays, has unfortunately stimulated others besides
Ireland to concoct some of the missing information ;
and in the last century a deliberate attempt was
made to pass off forged and falsified records as
genuine, by John Payne Collier (d. 1883), who from
1831 to at least 1853 issued Shakespearian books in
which a certain ' Perkin's Folio ' and Alleyn MSS. at
Dulwich were freely drawn upon, both of which
sources were demonstrably manufactured or tam-
pered with by insertion.

6. *Constantine Simonides*

The greatest forger of the last century was un-doubtedly Constantine Simonides, a Greek, who was born in 1824. To meet the requirements of modern critics, who know styles of writing, the colours of the ink and paints of different times, and the very kinds of parchment used, there is need of such a combina-tion of intellect with versatility, industry with ingenuity, as is rarely found. Yet, as even Juvenal could instance the audacity of the *Græculus esuriens*, so in modern times that mixed race has shown many of the qualities which, when perverted to a base use, produce the skilled forger. Simonides started by becoming a citizen of the world. From 1843 on, we find him successively on the shores of the Euxine, in Asia Minor, Thrace, Athos (where he wrote a hagiography), the Ægean, Cyprus, Alexandria, Cairo, Sinai (1844), Syria, Babylon, Persia, Russia, and Constantinople (in 1846). His next journeys were from Greece to Constantinople again, Odessa, St. Petersburg, and Germany ; then again to Egypt, the Ægean coasts, and finally to Liverpool (in 1853) and London. His stock-in-trade was a large number both of genuine MSS., obtained largely from Mount Athos, and of forged ones written by himself ; and his custom was to present first some genuine ones, and when his customer was off his guard, some of the second sort ; while he paid England and Germany the dubious compliment of selecting them as the field of his operations, as possessing either the largest amount of hard cash, or the greatest number of probable dupes.   Even in 1846 he is stated to have been in possession of 5000 MSS., which he exhibited to savants at Athens.

In 1854 and 1855, Simonides was well known at the British Museum and the Bodleian ; but Sir Frederick Madden extracted a considerable number of genuine MSS. from him at the former place, while Mr. Coxe, when asked his opinion of the date of some presented to him in Oxford, assigned them to the latter half of the nineteenth century.   In Sir Thomas Phillipps, however, Simonides found a less critical purchaser, and in the great Phillipps Library at Cheltenham are to be found some of the finest specimens of his powers in a Phocylides, an Anacreon, and a boustrophedon [1] Hesiod.

In 1855 he visited Berlin and Leipzig ; and when in July he met Wilhelm Dindorf, he informed him that he owned a Greek palimpsest, containing three books of records of the Egyptian kings, by Uranius of Alexandria, son of Anaximenes.   Dindorf offered a large price for it, but Simonides loftily replied that he intended to publish it first himself, and then to give the original to the library at Athens.   By persistence, however, Dindorf obtained temporary

---

[1] Βουστροφηδόν (boustrophēdon, ' in the manner in which an ox turns ') describes an ancient method of writing, in which the first line was written from left to right, the second from right to left, the third as the first, and so on : just as an ox in ploughing traces each successive furrow in an opposite direction to the preceding one.

possession of the precious palimpsest, and sent it to
Berlin, where it deceived all the members of the
Academy except Humboldt ; and the King of
Prussia offered £700 for the seventy-one leaves.
Further, Dindorf's representations induced the
Clarendon Press at Oxford to take up the treatise,—
and, indeed, it could hardly have done otherwise,—
and actual specimens were printed, with a preface
by Dindorf, and early in 1856 published. Only
seven copies were sold, besides the eleven sent to the
delegates of the Press, when the news came that
Uranius was a most uncelestial forgery. It was
found—(1) that the ancient writing of Uranius was
on the top of the later twelfth century writing, as
could clearly be seen by the help of a microscope ;
(2) that the Greek was far from correct [1] ; and (3)
that the coincidence between the most recent views
of Lepsius and other Berlin Egyptologists and the
new-found treatise was a little too striking. After
this, Uranius was very little heard of ; but Simonides
continued to be in evidence, for he was put on his
trial at Leipzig to answer two distinct charges—that
he had stolen the MS. from the Turkish Royal
Library ; and that he had forged it himself. To the
first he triumphantly replied that, if it was stolen,
it was at least not a forgery ; that they were bound
to show in what library and in what catalogue it was
marked as missing ; and, finally, that the Turks had
no libraries, and did not know what they were. To

---

[1] Κατ' ἐμὴν ἰδέαν represented ' in my opinion,' and so on.

the second plea he replied by a threat, which must have carried conviction to the dullest of his judges, to the effect that, if they would prove it was a forgery, he would forthwith print, under his own name, the other works of Uranius which he possessed, and achieve fame as the cleverest of authors, by exhibiting a knowledge of details which reached far beyond existing evidence ! In the end he was banished from Saxony, a kingdom which he was probably, on other grounds, not unwilling to quit.

After this Simonides appeared only once with any prominence before the public, when in 1861 he boldly asserted that he himself had written the whole of the Codex Sinaiticus, which Tischendorf had brought in 1856 from the Monastery of St. Catherine on Mount Sinai. The statement was, of course, received with the utmost incredulity ; but Simonides asserted, not only that he had written it, but that, in view of the probable scepticism of scholars, he had placed certain private signs on particular leaves of the codex. When pressed to specify these marks, he gave a list of the leaves on which were to be found his initials or other monogram. The test was a fair one, and the MS., which was at St. Petersburg, was carefully inspected. Every leaf designated by Simonides was found to be imperfect at the part where the mark was to have been found. Deliberate mutilation by an enemy, said his friends. But many thought that the wily Greek had acquired through private friends a note of some imperfect leaves in the MS., and had made unscrupulous use of the information.

Certainly Simonides' work, as evidenced by the MSS. at Cheltenham, was careful and laborious to a very high degree ; but the absolute breakdown of his pretensions, and of those of his only successor in audacity, Shapira,—who in the year 1883 demanded £1,000,000 for an ancient fragment of the Hebrew Pentateuch containing an eleventh commandment, ' Thou shalt not hate thy brother,'—seem to show that it is now almost impossible to deceive permanently the trained scholars and palæographers who are to be found in Germany, France, and England.

7. *The Vrain-Lucas Forgeries*

The collection of autograph letters has a great and natural attraction for many persons. Instead of a single author's works in manuscript, the collector of autographs obtains specimens of the handwriting of any number of celebrities, who may belong to a period or nation or class in which he is specially interested, or may represent general fame. For him all who can write are authors, and his ambition is to obtain an *a. l. s.* (autograph letter signed), or at least a signature, of all who come within the scope of his designs. There is a chiromancy connected with handwritings as well as hands, and the possession of an important and unpublished letter of a notable personage not only stimulates our interest, but may contribute something, if only through a study of literary style and handwriting, to an appreciation of his character.

The most celebrated trial in connexion with literary forgeries is perhaps that of Vrain-Lucas in 1870, for the most unblushing manufacture of autograph letters. The chief interest attached to the dupe and not the forger, for M. Chasles, besides being a collector of autographs, was a celebrated geometrician, and a Member of the French Academy. It is hardly credible that Vrain-Lucas between 1861 and 1869 supplied M. Chasles with no less than 27,000 autographs, for which he received 140,000 francs. These included letters of Julius Cæsar, Cicero, Socrates, and Shakespeare, and six were from Alexander the Great to Aristotle ! After this we can receive with calmness the information that one was from Pontius Pilate to Tiberius, and one from Judas Iscariot to St. Mary Magdalene ! The cream of it was that nearly every letter was in modern French, and on paper, and that the watermark of the paper was in many cases a *fleur-de-lys*. However, M. Chasles was prepared to receive any number in addition, when a circumstance induced him to submit some of his collections to wiser men than himself. He was engaged in writing a book to prove that the discovery of the principle of gravitation was not due to Sir Isaac Newton, but to Pascal. Vrain-Lucas, knowing this, supplied him with a correspondence between Pascal and the Hon.

Robert Boyle, and finally between Pascal and
Newton himself, on the deepest questions of
geometry, although the latter was at the supposed
date just eleven years old. This was too interesting
to be concealed, and was accordingly exhibited with
pride to the Academy. But M. Prosper Faugère and
Sir David Brewster, who was a Foreign Correspon-
dent of the Academy, denounced the letters at once
on general grounds as a forgery, and after a short
investigation the whole edifice collapsed. To illustrate a scientific principle, a cup of coffee was
introduced in a letter, some years before coffee was
known in Paris. French letters of Galileo were
produced, though Galileo was never able to write
that language ; and in the end Vrain-Lucas was
brought to trial and condemned to imprisonment.
The only redeeming feature about the affair was
that, with the exception of a very few letters, the
whole of the forgeries had been purchased by M.
Chasles, and none escaped to disseminate the
deception.

The boldest attempt in modern times to prove
an accepted book to be a forgery is undoubtedly
that of Ross (1883) and Hochart (1890), who both
declared that the sole MS. of the early part of
Tacitus's immortal *Annals* (Books i.-vi.) was written
by Poggio Bracciolini, the Italian scholar of the
Renaissance. The MS. is generally believed to be
of the eleventh century, but it is well known (see

L

p. 32) that a revival of the style of that and (more
usually) the succeeding century did take place in the
fifteenth century ; and it is maintained that Poggio
had not only practice in the imitation of old writings,
but also opportunities in connexion with this
particular codex.   It is undoubtedly remarkable
that there is only one clear reference to any part of
the *Annals* before the fifteenth century, namely, that
Ruodolphus, a monk of Fulda in the ninth century,
mentions him as writing of the river Visurgis (*Annals*,
Books i. and ii.).   But it may be remembered that
Catullus also was entirely lost sight of for centuries
together, and except that one of his poems occurs in
a tenth century Anthology, depends altogether on
MSS. not written before the second half of the
fourteenth century.   As Furneaux, the most recent
editor of the *Annals*, and the only one who has had
to defend their genuineness, says, we ought to be
satisfied with a few clear instances of facts unknown
in the Middle Ages, mentioned only by Tacitus and
confirmed by more recent epigraphical discoveries.
Of these he gives a list, the nature of which can be
gathered from the following samples.   They may
seem insignificant, but it is their insignificance
which makes them for this special purpose of real
importance.   Nero, the eldest son of Germanicus, is
stated by Tacitus to have been espoused to a
daughter of Creticus Silanus.   An inscription, discovered since the time of Poggio, confirms this, and
supplies the name Junia.   Tacitus again especially

notes that Julia Augusta, in dedicating a statue to
Augustus, gave offence to Tiberius by placing her
name before his. The Prænestine Calendar confirms
the fact by giving the names in the same order.
There remains one extraordinary proof of a kind
hardly to be parallelled elsewhere. Tacitus writes
in one place, referring to a Frisian insurrection, *ad
sua tutanda digressis rebellibus* (the insurgents having
moved off to protect their own quarters); but
Ptolemy, who wrote in Greek only one generation
after Tacitus, must have had the *Annals* before him,
for in a list of towns in North Germany he gives the
name of one as Σιατουτάνδα (*Siatoutanda*), which
cannot be anything else than a mistaken idea that
sua tutanda was the name of a place. Ptolemy gives
the latitude and longitude of Siatoutanda !

It may be confessed, however, that it is only too
easy to prove that the Italian scholars of the
Renaissance were not altogether above deceit with
respect to classical authors ; for example, Leonardo
Bruni of Arezzo (Leonardus Aretinus), when he
believed he possessed the unique MS. of Procopius's
Greek treatise, *De bello Italico adversus Gothos gesto*,
promptly issued it, in a Latin dress, as his own
work, so that even when printed in 1470 it bore his
name as author, and brought him posthumous
fame for some years, until a second MS. of the
Greek work was found, and Leonardus was
deposed.

A curious instance of a supposed original with a

romantic story attached to it may fitly close this series of examples, and will illustrate as well as any other the means for detecting originals and copies. Among the Cotton MSS. at the British Museum is a grant by Eadred, in A.D. 949, of certain lands to the monastery of Reculver in Kent, the body of it as usual being in Latin, and the boundaries of the lands described in Old English. The whole deed and the numerous signatures of attesting witnesses are also, as usual before the twelfth century, in one and the same handwriting, without autograph attestations. But one of the signatures reads thus : ' Ego Dunstanus indignus abbas rege Eadredo imperante hanc kartulam dictitando composui et *propriis digitorum articulis perscripsi*' (' I, Dunstan, an unworthy abbot, at King Eadred's command drew up and composed this charter, and *wrote it throughout with my own finger-joints* '). Here we have a most interesting instance of a charter, not only in the words, but from the pen of the great Dunstan, the first in the line of English ecclesiastical statesmen. How much is our interest heightened when we look closely at the *indignus* of the document ! For beneath the first three letters are clearly visible the traces of *abb*, first written and then smudged out. So we can imagine the Abbot of Glastonbury, when he wrote out the charter and came to his own name, first writing *Ego Dunstanus abb*— and then, in a sudden access of humility, substituting *indignus* abbas.   What life it seems to put into the parchment, and how near we seem to draw to Dunstan himself !

Alas ! Truth is better than romance, however bare and cold that truth may seem to be. The incisive criticism of modern times cuts clean away this interesting story, by proving that this charter is a copy and not an original. The critic confesses that *abb* was written and blotted out ; but when he proceeds to read the document he finds the following sentence : ' Unde nobis uictus restat sine dubio certus defuictoque Dominus dixit ' (' From which source there remains to us a livelihood undoubtedly secure . . . the Lord said,' and a quotation from the Gospels follows). But what is *defuictoque* ? It may be doubted whether the solution would ever have been discovered, did there not exist at Canterbury another copy of this charter which gives us the

clue. There the clause reads—' . . . de quo . . .,'

(gloss above: s. uictu)

showing that *de quo* was written (' about which'), and that then to explain the *quo* there was written above the word ' s(cilicet) uictu,' which forms what is called a gloss on *quo*. This gloss the scribe of the British Museum document tried to incorporate in the text, mistaking the ſ of s(cilicet) for f, and otherwise blundering until the *defuictoque* was produced ! Now *Dunstan* could not conceivably have written this monstrous word.

But is the Canterbury document in Dunstan's own hand ? No, not even that ; it also is a copy of the original, which itself has no doubt perished. The proof is that, in the Old English boundaries a clause is omitted through homoioteleuton (see p. 72), which Dunstan could not have omitted without being presently corrected. It need hardly be said that the accidental omission of *indignus* before abbas is not found in the Canterbury deed.

It has to be confessed, therefore, that if the work of Dunstan's ' own finger-joints ' does anywhere remain to us, it is not in the charter of Eadred, but in the words inscribed on the picture of Dunstan at the feet of Christ now in the Bodleian, figured at p. 105 of vol. i. of the illustrated edition of J. R. Green's *Short History of the English People*.[1]

This chapter has only attempted to deal with a few typical and famous falsifications, and has deliberately passed over a countless host, such as the Donation of Constantine (by which that Emperor surrenders important rights to the Bishop of Rome and his successors, and which was thoroughly believed in through the Middle Ages, and mourned over by Dante) ; the travels of Sir John Mandeville in the fourteenth century ; the *Antiquitates* of Johannes Nannius of Viterbo, 1498 ; the Casket Letters of Mary Queen of Scots (which are still believed in by some historians, and when produced from their silver box and declared to be autograph

---

[1] It may be noted that in this edition of Green's *History* there are a large number of illustrations from celebrated manuscripts, and not a few coloured copies of illuminations.

love-letters of the Queen, formed a weighty part of the evidence against her) ; the ' Εἰκὼν βασιλική, or Portraiture of His Majesty's [Charles I.'s] Sufferings ' (now ascertained to have been written by Bishop Gauden, though professing to be the King's retrospect of his own life, and intended to cause a revulsion of popular feeling in his favour at his trial, but accidentally delayed till about the time of his death), and the Poems of Ossian (pretended by Macpherson in 1760-63 to be epics translated from the Gaelic, but which it is not wholly fair to class as forgeries, since they appear to be based on the floating traditional poetry of the Western Highlands). For a fuller account of these see *Literary Forgeries*, by J. A. Farrer, 1907. But enough have been described to exhibit the salient features of this class of fraud, the extraordinary ingenuity and industry expended on them, the correspondence of the matter falsified with the needs and expectations of the time, the curious complexity of motives which the circumstances of their production lay bare, motives in which vanity and greed play a large part ; and the almost inevitable detection which, at least in these critical and reflective days, awaits the person who tries to impose on the world a concocted literary composition. Yet it has to be confessed that about twenty-five years ago, letters of Mary Queen of Scots, letters of Jacobite leaders, inedited poems of Burns, letters by Sir Walter Scott, and the like, some of which are undoubtedly spurious and many more probably so, were scattered far and wide by public sale in England and Scotland, having been found, as there seems no reason to doubt, in the secret drawer of an old cabinet where the original forger may have placed them. When this could take place before our eyes, it is premature to say that the book of successful literary fraud is closed.

CHAPTER X

LET us suppose that a private collector has purchased a MS. at some sale, that it has just reached
him, and that he is inexperienced in the treatment
of such volumes. Let us further assume, for the
sake of definiteness, that it is one of those very
common MSS., of which perhaps a hundred are sold
and bought every year in London auctions, lettered
outside ' Missale Romanum,' described (it may be)
in the catalogue as ' Breviarium,' and in reality a
Latin book of Hours (*Horæ*). How should the
owner proceed to investigate and treat it ? The
natural order of dealing with it is perhaps to consider
in turn its contents, its age, its state, and the best
way to catalogue or describe it.

1. *Contents*

No MS. written before the invention of printing
has a title-page. The volume presented may bear
on its first page a rubric beginning, ' Incipit . . .' or
' Incipiunt Hore Beate Marie Virginis ' ; but more
usually the title, if there is any, will be found on the
last page, in some such form as ' Expliciunt Hore

secundum usum Curie Romane, scripte per me
Willelmum de Gorham canonicum de Bridlington
anno incarnacionis dominice MCCCXLVJ. Gracias Deo.
Amen.' If these distinctive rubrics fail, how shall
we distinguish between the three cardinal kinds of
ordinary liturgical books, Missals, Breviaries, and
books of Hours ?

A Missal, which corresponds to the Communion
Service of the Church of England, may be detected
very quickly by searching for the Canon of the
Mass. This is the invariable part of the book, and
has not appreciably altered for 1500 years. It
begins with the words ' Te igitur,' and this particular
T is hardly ever an ordinary letter, but either
treated finely as a capital letter, or interwoven in a
splendid picture of the crucifixion, forming itself the
cross. Unfortunately, since the leaf containing this
illumination was often the finest in the volume, it has
occasionally been abstracted ; but words belonging
to the service of the Mass can usually be distinguished, while such rubrical words as Introitus,
Offertorium, Communio, Post-communio, are proper
to a Missal. A Gradual contains only the musical
portions of a Missal, as an Antiphoner does of a
Breviary, and can be distinguished by the musical
notes, and the omissions.

A Breviary may be said to correspond to a
Common Prayer Book with Proper Lessons, omitting
the Communion Service and the Occasional Offices.
It falls into six parts, which ought to be recognizable

with or without the rubrics in any ordinary volume :
—1. The *Calendar*, with rubrics and tables. 2. A
Psalter, with the versicles and responses of the week-
day Hours (see below), sometimes with small Offices
appended (this is equivalent to, but has never
received the title of, Commune de Tempore). 3.
Proprium de Tempore, collects and lections for
particular Sundays and week-days. 4. *Proprium
de Sanctis*, the same for particular Saints' Days. 5.
Commune Sanctorum, the same for Saints who have
no special service assigned to them. 6. Small
Offices, such as for dedications, commemoration or
burial of the dead, the Hours of the Virgin, etc.
Often the mere bulk of the volume will show that it
is a Breviary and not a book of Hours ; often its
division into two parts, for summer and winter (*pars
æstivalis, pars hiemalis*).

A book of Hours is usually in some form or other
the Horæ Beatæ Mariæ Virginis. There are two
Offices of the Virgin, one, the greater, often found in
the latter part of a Breviary ; one, the lesser, usually
found in books of Hours. The ordinary composition
of this lesser Office, which is properly for the use,
not of the priest as such, but of the laity, is as
follows, the usual subjects of the accompanying
illuminations being enclosed in brackets :—1. Calendar (emblems or scenes suited to each month).
2. Four lessons from the Gospels (the four evangelists
or their emblems), followed by some preliminary
prayers. 3. The Hours proper, that is to say, the

order of the service for each of the Canonical Hours, each consisting essentially of preparation, hymn, psalms, lections (i.e., lessons), hymn, canticle, prayers, but subject to special lengthening and shortening. The Hours are Matins, *ad Matutinas* (Annunciation) ; Lauds, *ad Laudes* (Visitation of Elizabeth) ; Prime, *ad Primam* (the Nativity) ; Tierce, *ad Tertiam* (Angels appearing to the Shepherds) ; Sext, *ad Sextam* (the Magi) ; None, *Ad Nonam* (Presentation in Temple) ; Vespers, *ad Vesperas* (Flight into Egypt) ; and Compline, *ad Completorium* (Coronation or Assumption of the Virgin). The Psalms and more usual prayers, hymns, versicles, etc., are often only indicated by their first few words. 4. The Penitential part, consisting of the seven Penitential Psalms (David praying, or David and Bathsheba) and a Litany with prayers. 5. The Office for the Dead, or strictly the choir-service part of the Office, the actual Mass being in the Missal. This choir-service consisted of special vespers and matins, called respectively from the first words of the antiphons to the first Psalm, ' Placebo ' and ' Dirige ' (funeral, day of judgment, etc.). 6. Private and miscellaneous prayers. This is the simplest analysis and the commonest order of a book of Hours, which corresponds to the Offices for Morning and Evening Prayer in the Church of England. Sometimes other Hours are found inserted after the fourth part, such as Hours of the Holy Cross, *Horæ Sanctæ Crucis* (with illuminations of the crucifixion) ; Hours of the Holy Spirit, *Horæ de Sancto Spiritu* (Pentecost) ; but in these cases the barest skeleton is given, showing just the parts in which such Hours differ from the precedent Hours of the Virgin.

Among the more important liturgical books which may be met with are, the Antiphoner (*Antiphonarium*, containing the musical parts of the Breviary), the Hymnary (*Hymnarium*), the *Legenda* (longer lessons from the Bible, books of sermons, and lives of Saints), the *Collectarium* (shorter lessons, with their Collects or short prayers), the Processional (*Processionale*, services during the frequent processions to or from an altar, round a church or cathedral, etc.) *Epistolaria* and *Evangeliaria* (containing the Epistles and Gospels of the Mass), the Gradual (*Gradale*, containing the musical part of the Missal), the *Manuale* (usually called on the Continent *Rituale*, comprising the Occasional Services, which, when they were such as only a bishop could perform, were written in the *Pontificale*), and the *Ordinale* (containing the rules for the proper sequence of the parts of a service). A *Primer* is the ordinary Hours of the Virgin with English rubrics, and often with English prayers, the amount of English varying very greatly in different primers. The *Portiforium* is only the term used commonly in England for the book elsewhere called a Breviary, while a *Sacramentary* is an early form of Missal before it included the Epistles and Gospels.

It is hardly possible to give more help towards identifying the contents of a book, but in the case of a charter or deed the analysis given on p. 174 will be useful. For other assistance recourse must be had to a librarian or to works of reference.

2. *The Age and Place of Writing*

After the subject of a MS. has been ascertained, the commonest question asked is, When was it written ? Unfortunately no part of manuscript lore is more difficult to learn or to impart to others when learnt than the determination of the age of a MS. Not only have many converging lines of evidence to be considered,—the character of the writing, the details of letters, the style of illumination, the look of the parchment, the binding, the known circumstances of its history,—but empirical rules have a way of breaking down. It may be that two MSS. written in the same year are presented to us, one by a scribe in extreme old age with conservative habits, and the other by a young copyist of the newest school. The style of these two would probably appear to differ by at least fifty years. Nothing but a course of palæography such as is adumbrated in Chapter III. will teach a student the way to arrive at a correct judgment ; on the other hand, it is wonderful to what insight experienced librarians may attain. The thing not to do is to venture rashly on too precise a statement, or, as

Waagen, to mistake the word *isto* on an illumination for 1530 ! I have known a person who, when engaged on dating a MS., asserted that a particular form or contraction in it was not found before 1424, and another not after 1430 ! The minimum of labour by which a collector could acquire sufficient information to date a volume between A.D. 500 and 1600 would be to compare in detail a set of facsimiles such as are supplied by Wattenbach or Arndt or Steffens or the Palæographical Society, and to study the article on ' Palæography ' by Sir Edward Maunde Thompson for the *Encyclopædia Britannica*, or the same author's longer *Introduction to Greek and Latin Palæography*.

With respect to localization, the answer to the question, *Where* a MS. was written, considerable progress has been made of late years, and it is in this direction that the most fruitful results may be expected. It may be doubted, as has already been pointed out (p. 44), whether any scriptorium was without its peculiar difference, whether of style or illumination. Take a Canterbury MS., and you can usually tell whether a monk of St. Augustine's or a monk of its great rival Christ Church wrote it. The Austin Canons, for instance, were fond of a sloping line as an edge to the long up or down strokes of such letters as b or p. The Christ Church monks had no such predilection, but were fond of appending a little upward tick (') to mark the beginning of an m or n or i, and such examples can be multiplied.

The broken-backed letters and peculiar orthography
of St. Alban's have also already been mentioned.

3. *Condition*

Is the MS. complete ?   Have any leaves dropped
out or been abstracted ?   This question can only be
certainly answered by an examination of each section
(see p. 15) of the book.   Turn the leaves over till
you discern a thread lying close to the back at the
extreme inner edge of the inner margin of a page ;
then turn over a few leaves, usually eight, till you
come to the next thread ; half-way between the two
threads, if the book is uniformly made up, will be the
end of one section and the beginning of another,
often slightly gummed together.   By continuing
this process you will soon discover if the MS. is
composed of sections of eight leaves (quaternions),
or six or twelve, or whatever it may be.   Then
simply verify each section to make sure it is complete.
Possibly there may be a signature (such as I, II,
III, etc.) on the first or last page of each section to
help one, or as in printed books, b i, b ii, b iii and the
like, or perhaps catchwords to mark the transition
from one section or leaf to another ; but even without these a leaf can hardly be absent without causing
a section to consist of an odd or unusual number of
leaves—which should at once arrest the attention.

Next, is the binding firm ?   Is it the original
binding ?   Are there book-worms in it ?   The first
point needs simple inspection ; and if the stitches are

giving way, or the board sides are broken, a binder's aid should be called in, who should be carefully instructed to destroy nothing of the old binding ; every written title along the back, every auction sale label, every piece of writing, should be preserved ; and if the back has to be renewed, the surface of the old back should be pasted on the inside of one of the sides. The second point needs a knowledge of the history of binding ; but if the sides are composed of boards covered with leather stamped even with simple lines and devices, they are well worth preserving, whatever their date. The third point, the presence of book-worms, is easily settled. If there are small round holes, where book-worms have been, hold the volume up so that any fine dust in the holes would drop out, and tap it with the fingers. If dust does fly out, the worms are alive and have been lately at work, and a further close inspection will probably show a white worm about a quarter of an inch long, or, if the season be summer or autumn, the small, brown-winged beetles (*Anobium domesticum* or *striatum*). The volume should then be put in an airtight box with a saucer of strong benzine and left for a night, at the end of which the animals will be dead. The worm lives, not on the pages of a volume, but on the paste of the binding ; and it is the irony of fate that the insect should object quite as much as the possessor of the volume to its self-imposed task of boring a tunnel to connect two happy feeding-grounds.

M

Finally, every part of the back, edges, sides, and fly-leaves of a MS. should be searched for indications of its history. The very strips of vellum, sometimes found under the thread in the centre of a section, inserted to prevent the thread from wearing the sides of the hole through which it passes, may yield fine proof of the *provenance* of the binding and of the volume.

4. *Cataloguing*

The description of a MS. should consist of three parts—(1) The technical description ; (2) the list of contents ; (3) the history and present shelf-mark.

The technical description, though it will be understood that the extent and arrangement of a catalogue entry are fairly matters of opinion, should include the language, the material, the date, the size, the number of leaves, the fact of illuminations, of imperfection, or of injury, and a note of the kind of binding, if remarkable. The size had better be reckoned by the minimum length and breadth of the inside of a box in which the book would just closely lie, and the height should always precede the breadth. It is more correct, but very unsatisfactory in practice, to measure the actual size of the average or largest leaf in the book ; and in favour of the rule here advocated, it may be remembered that if the binding is secure and firm, it is unlikely that it will have to be renewed, and your measurements altered, for many years to come. Every MS. must be foliated ; that is to say, every leaf, not page, marked with a consecutive number. The only safe rule is to lift the front cover of a volume, and to begin steadily at the upper right-hand corner of the fly-leaf which meets you, and so to go on marking every leaf (and, if some pieces of paper are pasted on a leaf, first the leaf and then each piece of paper), or, in the case of many blank-leaves together, every fifth or tenth, to the very end, appending ' ult.' to the last number. Then no abstraction of a leaf can possibly take place without detection. If you have missed foliating a leaf, say after fol. 25, mark 25 as 25^a, and the omitted one as 25^b (ult.) ; if a very faulty foliation has preceded you, put your own foliation at the *lower* right-hand corner, independently. Never send the volume away, even to the binder, till the whole is foliated. If, when a volume of say 293 leaves comes back from binding, there are four new fly-leaves at the beginning and end, mark the former i, ii, iii, iv (ult.), and at the end carry on your old foliation, describing the number of leaves as iv + 297. For describing illuminations, reserve the word ' miniature ' for a scene or figure, keeping illuminations as a general term, covering both miniatures and coloured capitals or rubrics.

The contents should be divided and described according to the circumstances ; see the typical example given below. As a rule, use English (unless special circumstances, such as the probable use of your catalogue in foreign countries, make

Latin desirable ; and certainly Latin is admirably
adapted for terse and accurate description), but
wherever possible use the actual words of the volume
with inverted commas. Number each division, and
mention the leaf on which it begins, ' fol. 14ᵛ,'
meaning the back or *verso* of leaf 14, and ' fol. 14,'
or, if necessary for distinctness, ' fol. 14ʳ,' the
front or *recto*. The extent of the description must
depend on the scope of your catalogue ; but in all
cases of anonymous works, the first few words should
be cited. Very often a few general words of description prefixed to the first division of the contents
saves repetition, and makes the information clearer.
A separate paragraph may be given to a description
of illuminations or other striking features.

Lastly, the history, so far as known from internal
or external evidence, should be succinctly told, and
the successive shelf-marks which the book has borne
under different owners.

A collector is no doubt, in ordinary cases, subject
to certain weaknesses, such as a gradual tendency to
lose his power of discrimination, and thus to ac-
cumulate instead of selecting, and to buy and not
use ; a refined form of selfishness which makes him
nervous if any one else wants to see or use his books ;
a plethora of unrealizable schemes for publishing the
contents of his volumes ; a secret hope that his own
books are altogether unique (as in the case of that
Frenchman who, hearing that a friend had a second
copy of a printed book which he had deemed his

unique possession, set fire to his friend's house, and
burnt owner and book together). But all may be
reasonably forgiven, if the possessor of a collection
will only print a catalogue of it.

The collector would also do a great service to the
readers of his catalogue by making use of photography to represent pages of some of the treasures
which he is describing. The processes of collotype
(which preserves the appearance even of the surface
of the parchment) and photo-lithography (which is
rather less expensive, and is similar to an engraving
in being simply a black design printed on the white
surface of paper) are now rapidly becoming cheap-
ened, so that with a small expenditure the catalogue
can be immensely improved in interest and permanent value. Colour printing is also being wonder-
fully improved, and colour-photography is in active
progress towards success. For some purposes
bromide prints, or even (for collation) rotographs
(a *single* copy with white writing on a dark background, very inexpensive) are sufficient.

The following may be given as a typical (fictitious)
catalogue entry on the principles just laid down :—

XVII

In Latin, on parchment ; written in the second half of the
fifteenth century in England ; 6¼ × 4½ inches, iii + 157 leaves ;
with illuminated capitals and four full-page miniatures ; in part
imperfect, see below.

Poems of Virgil, etc. :—

1. (fol. 3) The Georgics, from ii. 120 to end, some
leaves being lost at the beginning.

2. (fol. 60ᵛ) ' Incipit Expositio Seruij grammatici in libros Vergilij Bucolicon et Georgicon.'

3. (fol. 75) The Æneid.

(Description of the miniatures.)

On fol. 155v, ' Qui me scribebat Gulielmus nomen habebat.' ' John Rousham oweth this book ' (early 16th century). In the Graham sale (1834) this volume was no. 1415 and sold for 15s. Now MS. Collier 17.

CHAPTER XI

PUBLIC AND PRIVATE RECORDS

THE desire to study the history, either of the place in which we live or the family we represent, is natural only to the minority who think of the past at all. As Bishop Stubbs says : ' It is really a curious thing that, in days in which the doctrine of heredity is taking its place as a scientific axiom, men should flatter themselves that they are self-made, and not care to explore what their ancestors did for them.' But this minority will in the future, we may be sure, rapidly increase in numbers, and even now it is worth while to devote some pages to their interests. For many do not in the least know how to begin their research ; and until some elements of palæography are learnt, there is a feeling of distaste, not unmingled with a sort of dread, when original records are first placed before them. The manuscripts appear so bare and strange, divested of the explanatory setting in which they are placed in our printed histories, and at first sight so odd and unreadable, not to say worn and dirty. Yet there is no better or more bracing exercise for a student of history than to work through for himself a Court Roll or Inquisition, or even an ordinary Deed of Gift

of a period in which he is interested. It is original,
and not dressed up in modern apparel with introduction and notes : it is as the men of that day left
it, in absolute integrity. And there are few better
tests of intellect than the endeavour to see the
' points,' the bearing of isolated facts, the relative
importance of details, presented to us in an original
document. The present chapter will give an outline
of the commonest kinds of English record other than
chronicles, letters, and set literary productions. We
will begin with Public Records, and only premise that
it is a well-considered rule that researchers should
first make use of all printed information before they
systematically explore manuscript sources.

England is quite exceptional in the extent and
continuity of her historical documents. No nation
can show a book which can range with Domesday
Book, the grandest and among the earliest of English
records. The two volumes of the work, now preserved in the Public Record Office, contain a survey
of all England, except Northumberland, Cumber-
land, Westmoreland, and Durham, made in A.D.
1085-1086, of which no better account can be given
than what we find in the almost contemporary Old
English Chronicle (see p. 117), of which a translation
follows :—

' A.D. MLXXXV. . . . After this the king [William the
Conqueror] had a great council, and very deep speech about
this land, how it was peopled, or by what men ; then sent
his men all over England, into every shire, and caused to be
ascertained how many hundred hides were in the shire, or

what land the king himself had, and cattle within the land,
or what dues he ought to have in twelve months from the
shire. Also he caused to be written how much land his
archbishops had, and his suffragan bishops, and his abbots,
and his earls; and—though I may narrate somewhat
prolixly—what or how much each man had who was a
holder of land in England, in land or in cattle, and how much
money it might be worth. So very narrowly he caused it to
be traced out, that there was not one single hide, nor one
virgate of land, nor even—it is shame to tell, though it
seemed to him no shame to do—an ox, nor a cow, nor a
swine, was left that was not set down in his writ. And all
the writings were brought to him afterwards.'

A specimen of a single, almost random, entry may
be given, also translated :—

'The king holds Windsor in demesne. . . . Of the land of
this manor, Albert the clerk holds one hide and a half, and a
third part of one dene ; Walter, son of Other, holds one hide
and a half and one virgate, and as much woodland as will
serve five hogs for pannage (food). Gislebert Maminot
holds three virgates, William Belet one hide, Aluric one hide,
and another Aluric half a hide, and the priest of the town one
hide and a half, and two sergeants of the King's Court half
a hide, and Eudo the steward two hides. In the time of
King Edward it was worth 15 pounds, and afterwards 7
pounds, now 15 pounds.'

Domesday has always been held of primary
authority in courts of law, and no appeal from it is
ever allowed. Before it, our chief authorities for the
history of land are separate charters in Latin or Old
English ; but from Domesday onward there is a
series of full and accurate public documents, the
chief kinds of which are as follows.

Knights' Fees (Feoda Militum) were lands—at first

about 6,000 in number—held of the king by barons, bishops, monasteries, and the like, with the duty of supplying a certain number of knights, fully equipped, for the king's service. Inquisitions were held from time to time, to ascertain the exact indebtedness of the holders of these fees, and some of these returns are known by distinct titles, as the Black Book of The Exchequer (*Liber Niger Scaccarii*, A.D. 1166), the Red Book of the Exchequer, Scutage Rolls, and the Testa de Neville (about 1250).

Pipe Rolls (supposed to be so called because from their size and the manner of folding them they looked like long pipes) begin in A.D. 1131, and contain the details of the revenues of the Crown, according to counties, not merely from land, but from every source, together with the public expenditure.

But it is in post-Norman times, from A.D. 1154, that the information becomes really full and un-broken. In the *Patent Rolls* (so called because they were despatched open, *rotuli patentes*, as being of a public nature) we find recorded all grants of lands and honours, all pensions and privileges, given by the king to individuals or corporate bodies. The *Close Rolls* (which were delivered closed up, *rotuli clausi*, as of a more private nature, or addressed to two or three persons only) are in reality almost as wide in their range as the Patent Rolls, dealing, for instance, with the wardship of minors, mining rights, orders to sheriffs, homage, and treasure trove. It is estimated that the Close Rolls alone, if printed, would fill 450 volumes of 1000 octavo pages each. The *Hundred Rolls*, of A.D. 1274, are of great importance for local history, containing an inquisition into the state of every hundred (a division of a county), and answers, on oath, to questions on all points that had reference to the public exchequer. They contain about 70,000 personal names, and were followed by other similar sets. The *Placita de Quo warranto* are a sequel of the Hundred Rolls, and are answers to the question, *Quo warranto ?* (by what right do you act ?), asked by the king's officers of all who were supposed to have done wrong, or to have not done right, in matters touching the Royal rights and revenues, while the king himself was away at the Crusades. *Inquisitiones post mortem* were inquiries by a local jury, after a death, to determine, where there was doubt, of what lands the deceased was possessed, on what terms of service, and who the next heir was. *Inquisitiones ad quod damnum* were held in case of a licence being applied for to alienate lands, and answered the query, " Does it injure the Crown, or any one, if the licence is granted ? ' (*Ad quod damnum ?* ' To what injury does it tend ? '). There might be a licence needed to build a new mill, and the question would arise, is it too near another ? Would it injure the fishery or river rights to have a new weir ? and the like. *Pedes Finium* (' feet of fines ') is the title of a large and splendid series of records, which gives a summary (usually written at the *foot* of the original) of a *final* agreement (which usually began, *Hæc est finalis concordia*, ' This is the final agreement '), thus preserving the essential parts of the document without the interminable series of formal phrases and repetitions in the complete deed.

The above are perhaps the chief classes of our general public records, such as may be consulted in the Public Records Office in London ; but one may mention also the Coroners' Rolls (in cases of accident or sudden death) ; the Registers of Law Courts, such as the Courts of Chancery, King's Bench, Common Pleas, and Exchequer ; the Escheat Rolls (accounts of property which has lapsed to the Crown) ; and, last not least, Parliamentary documents and State papers. So, too, every town has, or might have had, its municipal books, recording council meetings, admissions of freemen and apprentices, and public accounts. But one class of special documents deserves a fuller account, namely, those connected with the clergy and religious establishments. After Domesday we find an invaluable return, in A.D. 1291, called the *Taxatio Ecclesiastica*, a valuation in detail of all ecclesiastical property, because a tenth of such revenues had been granted by Pope Nicholas IV. to Edward I., for six years, to defray the expenses of a Crusade. And at the time of the Reformation there was naturally a *Valor Ecclesiasticus*, which showed Henry VIII. exactly what the Crown received, in lieu of the Pope, in such matters as first-fruits and tenths. Finally, the rolls of the *Court of*

Augmentation dealt with the property of suppressed religious houses. Every large monastery had its Chartulary (or collection of charters copied out at full length into a large volume), and generally its Register or Chronicle, in which general and local history were found in one chronological series ; and every diocese had its registers of ecclesiastical affairs, disputed rights, and admissions to incumbencies, beginning, in the case of Lincoln, as early as A.D. 1217. Churchwardens' Accounts (from the fifteenth century) and Parish Registers (from A.D. 1538, or more usually from 1558, but often neglected or lost [1]) afford endless material for the history of villages, manors and families. All these, and many other classes which might be mentioned, are public, or have a public side ; let us now turn to those which may, by comparison, be termed private.

2. *Private or Personal Records*

There are four conspicuous kinds of document which may be put under this head,—deeds or agreements, wills, visitations of heralds, and manor- or court-rolls.

A deed by which two parties agree about the disposal of something of value is the most general document known, and in its form, so far as the matter will allow, fairly constant. It generally consists of

[1] The Census returns for 1831 contain a list of all the parish registers then existing.

the following eleven parts, usually before the Reformation written in Latin, which put together make up a complete typical deed :—

1. Introduction.

   Sciant præsentes et futuri quod ego (or, if a Royal grant, Henricus Dei gratia rex Angliæ Hiberniæ et Franciæ omnibus ad quos præsentes literæ pervenerint salutem. Noveritis quod nos . . . , or the like).

2. Grantor's name.

   Robertus Godifere.

3. Act of gift.

   Dedi et concessi et hac præsenti charta mea confirmavi.

4. Grantee's name.

   Henrico de La Birch et heredibus suis.

5. The thing granted.

   Unam peciam terræ (often with long and accurate description of the property, especially with reference to adjacent properties).

6. Quality of gift (usually ungrammatical).

   Habendum et tenendum predictam peciam terræ cum omnibus pertinentiis suis prædicto Henrico libere quiete bene et pace imperpetuum.

7. Consideration, rent, etc.

   Reddendo inde mihi et heredibus meis unum obolum redditus annuatim die Lunæ proximo post festum sancti Michaëlis.

8. Warranty.

   Et ego Robertus et heredes mei warrantizabimus predictam peciam terræ contra omnes homines.

9. Sealing.

   In cujus rei testimonium tam sigillum meum quam sigillum prædicti Henrici huic scripto indentato alternatim sunt appensa.

10. Witnesses.

    His testibus, Radulpho de Woodstock, Rogero de Toeni, Hugone filio Roberti cum multis aliis.

11. Date.

Datum die Veneris proximo post dominicam Quasimodo [1] *anno regni Regis Henrici post conquestum quarti septimo.*

From this type variations of course occur, according as the deed is a certificate or notice of a fact, a confirmation (in which the grant or grants confirmed are often quoted at full length, preceded by the words ' inspeximus chartam in hæc verba ' [' we have seen a charter in these terms '], whence the name ' inspeximus ' applied to confirmations), a covenant in which both parties have duties to perform, an exchange, a final concord (see p. 172), a letter of attorney (appointing an agent to act on behalf of one party), a writing obligatory (recording a duty or debt, and binding the debtor to fulfil his obligation under penalty), a release (giving up a right), or other forms known to lawyers. An exemplification means simply an official copy of a deed. Some other common terms met with in the description of deeds are Feoffment or Infeoffment (putting a person in possession of a thing), grants in Frankalmoigne (donations *in francam elymosinam,* ' as free alms,'

---

[1] Sundays were often designated by the first word or words of the introit with which the Mass began on that day, as *Ad te levavi* (Advent Sunday), *Oculi* (the third Sunday in Lent), and others. *Quasimodo* was the first Sunday after Easter, the introit beginning ' Quasi modo geniti infantes ' (1 Pet. ii. 2). The date of this (fictitious) deed would therefore be Friday, April 23, 1406. As an example of the nicety sometimes required in computing a date, the following may be adduced :—' Datum die Lunæ proximo ante Nativitatem Sancti Johannis Baptistæ anno regni Regis Ricardi post conquestum secundi secundo : ' the solution of which is given in the index under *Date.*

usually to a religious house), indentures (when both
the grantor's copy of a deed with the grantee's seal
and the grantee's copy with the grantor's seal, were

written on one piece of parchment, thus :- [deed ⋮ deed] -o

and a curved or jagged line (*indentura*) was cut along
the line of dots, so that the two pieces could be for
ever identified as fitting precisely into each other
when brought together).

In ancient times personal signature was not required, and even the sign of the cross, by which
before the Conquest the signatories attested their
presence, was affixed by the scribe of the whole
deed ; in fact, not till the fourteenth century do we
find royal attestation, not till the fifteenth the
signature of a petitioner or party to a deed, and not
till the sixteenth actual autographs of witnesses. In
England after the Conquest we do not expect to find
deeds dated until after A.D. 1290 ; but, on the other
hand, undated ones after 1320 are hardly found at all.

Wills are among the most authentic materials of
personal history, often abounding in precise information of relationships, age, and condition. Though
private documents, they have from early times been
deposited or enrolled in various public offices, such
as those of the Prerogative Courts of Canterbury and
York. The former collection is now at Somerset
House in London, and extends back to the year
1383 ; the York wills go back to 1389 ; but there
are numerous lesser offices. Often the old registers

of a town contain early wills enrolled at the desire of the testator, in order to preserve the terms of the will from any tampering or possible loss.

Heraldic Visitations, which were held once in every generation in each county from 1530 to 1687, were due to the jealousy with which the right to bear arms was safeguarded. The Heralds' College or College of Arms was specially instituted to preserve this privilege, and to register all recent changes in the line of descent of families. The Visitations were personally conducted by heralds, and every change in or addition to pedigrees was investigated by reference to documents or by evidence on oath. The results were finally copied out and certified and sent up to the College of Arms, and still present the most certain pedigrees which we possess. They are classed with private records on account of their subject-matter.

One very interesting class of documents remains, the Court Rolls of a manor. The descent of the manor is usually the key to the history of a parish or village ; and where the Court Rolls are preserved, we have as clear a picture as can be obtained of the inner life and changes of a district.

It is important to bear in mind that there were two distinct Courts of law which were held within a manor. The first was the *Court Leet*, the King's Court, properly held by the Sheriff as representing the king, but usually allowed to be held by the tenants on payment of a sum called the Certum

N

Letæ. This Court was for public offences against the commonwealth, for felonies, and the like. The other Court was the *Court Baron* (Curia Baronis), or Court of the Lord of the Manor. This was local, and in it the customs of the particular manor prevailed ; the causes tried in it were offences against the said customs, personal squabbles, actions for non-payment of debts, for assault, for diverting roads, polluting streams, allowing cattle to trespass, brewing bad beer, and the numberless bickerings which prevent life from stagnating in rural districts. The jury were freemen from the manor itself, or at least from the tithing (decenna, whence their name of decennarii, tithing-men) within which the manor might be, and were presided over by the Steward of the Lord. The jury 'presented' certain facts, which were inquired into, and punishment meted out. Most amusing as well as interesting these glimpses of real life are to an observant eye ; the quaint solemnity of the proceedings, the simple offences, the fresh-air kind of justice done, the world-old yet modern kinds of men and women concerned. Take, for instance, an ordinary (translated) entry from a Court Roll of Cressingham in A.D. 1329 :—

> (Presentment) of Thomas Buteler for rescue from the servant of Alexander Nally of one pig taken in the corn of Alexander Nally.
> Of Alice Brun because she did not allow the ale-tasters to do their duty.
> Of Peter le Miller for a hue and cry justly raised upon him by the wife of William le Fuller.
> (The fines were 6*d*., 2*d*., and 6*d*. respectively.)

Or this from a Court Roll of Little Barton (in Suffolk, owned by Bury St.Edmund's), dated 1461 :—

> And they present that Sir Robert Loote, rector of the church there, did trespass on the meadow of the lord called Netemedowe with three horses. Therefore he is fined vj*d*.
>
> And that John Gooch with his cart, John Goodarde in the usual way, Richard Milton as before, and master Thomas Wellys with his cart, did make a wobbly track at Shakerspatch without a license, where they ought not. Therefore they are fined xij*d*. each.
>
> And that William Sopere did leap upon John Newman with a pitchfork, against the peace (" fecit insultum super Joh. Newman cum j pitchforke, contra pacem "). So he is fined iij*d*.

Human nature is recognizable as much in the matter of Essonia (excuses) for not coming to take part in the Court, as in any other part of these records. For there were five recognized excuses— 1. *Ultra mare*, ' I have gone abroad ; ' 2. *De Terra Sancta*, ' I am on my way to the Holy Land ; ' 3. *De malo veniendi*, ' I can't manage to come ; ' this was called the ' common excuse ; ' 4. *De malo lecti*, ' I am confined to my bed ; ' and 5. *De servitio Regis*, ' the king requires my services.'

It is a thousand pities that more care has not been and is not taken of Court Rolls. Few have been printed, and countless numbers have been destroyed from inability on the part of their owners to see the importance of them. Both they and parish registers should be preserved with all possible care.

' Hic locus est metæ : liber explicit, atque valete.'

APPENDIXES

PAGE

A. Public Libraries with more than 5000 MSS. - - - - 181

B. Chief Catalogues of MSS. in the British Museum, Bodleian and Cambridge University Libraries, etc. 184

C. Books useful for the Study of Manuscripts - - - - 195

APPENDIX A

PUBLIC LIBRARIES WHICH CONTAIN MORE THAN FIVE THOUSAND MANUSCRIPTS.

(Compiled partly (by leave) from H. R. Tedder's article on *Libraries* in various editions of the *Encyclopædia Britannica*, partly from *Minerva*, the *Literary Year Book* and similar sources ; but in many cases there is an absence of reliable data. F. W. Hall's Companion to Classical Texts (1913) gives a long and useful glossary of Latin names of collections of MSS. The present list must be regarded as tentative. For instance, American libraries possess millions of modern papers, but not many volumes of older MSS., in the sense in which the word is generally used in this treatise.)

GREAT BRITAIN AND IRELAND.

Cambridge—
  University Library, 9,000
London—
  British Museum, . 67,800
  (and 81,300 charters).
  Guildhall, . . 6,000
  India Office, . 15,000

Manchester—
  John Rylands, . 7,000
Oxford—
  Bodleian Library, . 40,000
  (and 20,000 charters, etc).

AUSTRIA AND HUNGARY.

Buda-Pesth—
  National Museum, . 16,000
Cracow, , . 8,400

Prag—
  Königl. Bibliothek, 5,000
Vienna—
  Königl. Bibliothek, 27,000

BELGIUM.

Brussels, ... 30,000

DENMARK.

Copenhagen—
  Kongelige Bibliothek, . 22,000
  Univ. Bibliothek, . . 6,500

FRANCE.

Grenoble, . .	10,000	Paris—
Lyons, . . .	5,300	Bibliothèque Maz-
Paris—		arine, . . 6,000
Bibliothèque de		Bibliothèque Na-
l'Arsenal, .	10,400	tionale, . . 111,000

GERMANY.

Berlin—		Leipzig—	
Königl. Bibliothek,	33,600	Univ. Bibliothek, .	6,000
Cassel—		Munich, . .	50,000
Murhardsche Bibl.	6,300	Strasbourg, . .	13,000
Dresden, . .	6,000	Stuttgart—	
Göttingen, . .	7,400	Königl. Bibliothek,	5,500
Gotha, . . .	7,000	Wolfenbüttel, . .	9,000
Hamburg, . .	8,000		

HOLLAND.

The Hague, . . .	6,000
Leyden, ...	6,400

ITALY.

Bologna, . . 6,000	Rome—	
Florence—	Biblioteca Casanatense	6,000
Biblioteca Nazionale, 22,000	Biblioteca Vaticana,	45,000
„ Medico-	Biblioteca Vittorio-	
Laurenziana, 9,900	Emmanuele,	6,200
Milan—	Siena, . . .	5,100
Biblioteca Am-	Venice—	
brosiana, . . 10,000	Biblioteca Marciana,	12,084
Naples—	Museo Civico Correr	11,000
Biblioteca Nazionale, 8,000	Vicenza, . .	6,000
Parma, . . . 5,000		

PORTUGAL.

Lisbon—
Biblioteca Nacional, . . 16,000

Russia.

Moscow, ...	7,500
St. Petersburg—	
Imperial Library, . .	34,000

Spain.

(Escorial, ...	5,000)
Madrid—	
Biblioteca Nacional, . .	20,000

Sweden.

Stockholm, . . 10,500 | Upsala, . . 14,000

Switzerland.

Bâle—	
Univ. Bibliothek, . .	5,200

The East.

Benares, . . .	6,000
Calcutta—	
Royal Asiatic Soc. of	
Bengal, . . .	20,000
Tanjur, ...	18,000

APPENDIX B

*LIST OF THE CHIEF OFFICIAL PRINTED CATA-
LOGUES OF MANUSCRIPTS IN EUROPEAN
LANGUAGES IN THE BRITISH MUSEUM, THE
BODLEIAN LIBRARY AT OXFORD, THE CAM-
BRIDGE UNIVERSITY LIBRARY, ETC.*

A.—BRITISH MUSEUM (see p. 93).

1. SLOANE (1753).

A catalogue of the manuscripts preserved in the
British Museum hitherto undescribed . . . including the collections of Sir Hans Sloane, Bart.
the Rev. Thomas Birch, D.D., and about five
hundred volumes . . . [acquired] at various
times. . . . By Samuel Ayscough. . . .

2 vols. : Lond. 1782, 4to.

The work is arranged by subjects, so that the
description of a miscellaneous MS. is to be found
in several different places, but there is an index of
pressmarks and of names. The MSS. are numbered 1-5017, of which 1-4100 are Sloane,
4101-4478 are Birch ; the rest are chiefly Madox,
Rymer, Milles, and Bankes MSS.

Catalogus librorum manuscriptorum bibliothecæ
Sloanianæ.

Lond. [about 1841], fol.

This is an incomplete unpublished book without
title-page, and dealing only with MSS. Sloane

184

1-1091, but is continued to No. 4014 in 9 'auto-graphed' folio volumes, not published. An index was published in 1904.
See below, ADDITIONAL MSS.

2. COTTON (1753).

A catalogue of the manuscripts in the Cottonian Library . . . [861 vols.].

Lond. 1802, fol.

By J. Planta. An appendix to this catalogue forms part of Casley's catalogue, see No. 4 below (pp. 313-45).

3. HARLEIAN (1753).

A catalogue of the Harleian manuscripts . . . [7639 vols.].

4 vols. : Lond. 1808-12, fol.

This was begun by Humphrey Wanley (1-2407), who died in 1726, and was continued by Casley (2408-5709), Hocker (5710-7355), F. Douce, and others, and edited by the Rev. R. Nares ; the index is by the Rev. T. H. Horne.

4. OLD ROYAL COLLECTION (1757).

A catalogue of the manuscripts of the King's Library. . . . By David Casley . . . [nearly 2000 vols.].

Lond. 1734, 4to.

A new catalogue in four volumes may be expected shortly.

5. LANSDOWNE (1807).

A catalogue of the Lansdowne manuscripts . . . [1245 vols.]. Lond. 1819, fol.

This was largely by Francis Douce, and completed and edited by Sir Henry Ellis.

6. HARGRAVE (1813).

A catalogue of manuscripts formerly in the possession of Francis Hargrave, Esq. . . . [499 vols.].

Lond. 1818, 4to.

Compiled by Sir Henry Ellis.

7. BURNEY (1818).

Catalogue of manuscripts in the British Museum. New Series. Vol. i. Part 1. The Arundel manuscripts [550 vols.]. Part 2. The Burney manuscripts [524 vols.]. Part 3. Index.

Lond. 1834-40, fol.

By the Rev. J. Forshall.

8. KING'S (OR NEW ROYAL) COLLECTION (1828) [446 vols.].

Of this there is no printed or published catalogue, but a manuscript one available to readers at the Museum.

9. EGERTON (1825), see ADDITIONAL MSS.

10. ARUNDEL (1831), see No. 7 (BURNEY) : the Arundel catalogue was issued in 1834, but the index not till 1840.

11. ADDITIONAL MSS.

This is the series in which all acquisitions are numbered if they are not sufficiently numerous or important to form a separate collection by themselves.

1-5017 have been mentioned above under Sloane.

5018-5027, 5214-5308 are also Sloane MSS.; and for these and all others between 5028 and about 7084, and for 4324-4326 B, there is only a catalogue in twenty-three folio volumes of manuscript kept in the Museum. For index, see below.

About 7084-8219 are contained (without any numbers assigned) in the three Annual Lists of Donations and Bequests, 1828-30, published in 1830 and 1831, 8vo ; but none of the purchased MSS. are here catalogued, though included in the numbering.

8220-8891, 8901 are in the ' List of Additions, 1831 ' (Lond. 1833, 8vo).

8892-8900, 8902 to about 9344, are in the ' List . . . 1832 ' (Lond. 1834, 8vo).

9346 to about 9707, with some earlier, are in the ' List . . . 1833 ' (Lond. 1835, 8vo).

9708 to about 9814 are in the ' List . . . 1834 ' (Lond. 1837, 8vo).

9821 to about 10,018 are in the ' List . . . 1835 ' (Lond. 1839, 8vo).

At this point comes in the ' Index to the Additional Manuscripts, with those of the Egerton Collection . . . acquired in the years 1783-1835 ' (Lond. 1849, fol.). This covers all the non-Oriental MSS. from 5018 to 10,018, but includes Hebrew. It is a rare volume, since by an error only 100 copies were printed.

10,019-11,748 with a few earlier are in the ' List of Additions to the Manuscripts . . . 1836-1840 ' (Lond. 1843, 8vo), with index.

11,749-15,667 are in the ' Catalogue of Additions to the Manuscripts . . . 1841-1845 ' (Lond. 1850, 8vo), with index.

Nos.	Accessions of	Published
15,668-17,277	1846-47	Lond. 1864, 8vo, with index.
17,278-19719	1848-53	Lond. 1868, 8vo, with index.
19,720-24,026	1854-60	Lond. 1875, 8vo.

Nos.	Accessions of	Published.
24,027-29,909	1854-75, vol. ii.	Lond. 1877, 8vo. An ' Index to the Catalogue . . . 1854-1875,' was published in 1880.
29,910-31,896	1876-81	Lond. 1882, 8vo, with index.
31,897-33,344	1882-87	Lond. 1889, 8vo, with index.
33,345-34,526	1888-93	Lond. 1894, 8vo, with index.
34,527-36,297	1894-99	Lond. 1901, 8vo, with index.
36,298-37,232	1900-05	Lond. 1907, 8vo, with index.
37,233-38,091	1906-10	Lond. 1912, 8vo, with index.

In almost all of the above catalogues are to be found gradually described—(1) The series of Egerton MSS. 1-607, with additions (purchased with funds left by the Earl of Bridgewater and Lord Farnborough) both of Egerton MSS. up to No. 2889, and of Egerton Charters and Rolls up to 621 ; (2) Additional Charters and Rolls 1-55,544 ; (3) Seals ; (4) Papyri, 1-1872. An index to the Charters and Rolls acquired up to 1900 was issued in 1901-12, 2 vols.

12. ASHBURNHAM (1883).

Catalogue of the manuscripts in the Stowe Collection. . . . By Mr. R. R. Knowles (reprinted from the Report of Royal Commission on Historical Manuscripts.)

Appendix No. 2 of *Papers relating to the Purchase of the Stowe Collection by Her Majesty's Government,* Lond. 1883, fol. Not official.

12. STOWE (1883).

Catalogue of the Stowe MSS., 2 vols. (Lond. 1895-6, 8vo), with index.

Also numerous Oriental Catalogues.

Besides the above, there are catalogues by subjects,
or kinds, as follows (see also *Birch*, p. 199) :—

Description of the Greek Papyri in the British
Museum, Part I. (By J. Forshall.)
> Lond. 1839, 4to.
> This includes 44 papyri.

Catalogue of the manuscript maps, charts, and
plans, and of the topographical drawings. . . .
(By John Holmes.)
> Vols. 1-2, Lond. 1844, 8vo.
> This contains Great Britain, Ireland, and
> France only.

Catalogo dos Manuscriptos portuguezes existentes
no Museu Britannico . . . Por Frederico Fran-
cisco de La Figanière . . . [with index.]
> Lisboa, 1853, 8vo. Not official.

Facsimiles of Ancient Charters in the British
Museum.
> 4 vols., Lond. 1873-78, fol. (vol. i. smaller),
> and a new series, vol. 1 (1903).

Deutsche Handschriften aus dem Britischen
Museum. In Auszügen herausgegeben von Dr.
Jacob Bæchtold. . . .
> Schaffhausen, 1873, 8vo.
> This does not pretend to be a complete collec-
> tion, and is not an official publication.

Catalogue of the manuscripts in the Spanish
language. . . . By Don Pascual de Gayangos.
> Vols. 1-4, Lond. 1875-93, 8vo.
> This has at present no index, but is arranged
> by subjects.

Catalogue of Ancient manuscripts in the British
Museum. Part I. Greek [with facsimiles].
Lond. 1881, fol.
————   Part. II. Latin [with facsimiles].
Lond. 1884, fol.

Catalogue of Romances in the department of
manuscripts. . . . By H. L. D. Ward. (Vol. 3
by J. A. Herbert).
Vols. 1-3, Lond. 1883-1910, 8vo.

Notes sur les Manuscrits grecs du British Museum,
par H. Omont (Extrait de la *Bibliothèque de
l'École des Chartes*, t. xlv.).
Paris, 1884, 8vo.
This gives a complete list of the references of
the 760 Greek MSS. in the Museum, with notes on
the scribes. Not official.

Catalogue of Seals, 6 vols. Lond. 1887-1900, 8vo.

Catalogue of the Greek Papyri in the British
Museum, edited by F. G. Kenyon, etc. Vols.
1-5.
Lond. 1893-1917, 4to, and 3 vols. of facsimiles,
fol.

Facsimiles of Autographs, 5 series.
Lond. 1896-1900, fol.

Illuminated MSS. (in colours), 4 series.
Lond. 1899-1903, fol.

Facsimiles of Biblical MSS.
Lond., 1900, fol.

Catalogue of MSS. relating to Wales, parts 1-2.
Lond. 1900-1903, 8vo.

Catalogue of the manuscript music. Vols. 1-3, by
A. H. Hughes.

Lond. 1906-1909, 8vo.

Reproductions from Illuminated MSS. (not
coloured), 3 series.

Lond. 1907-1908, 4to.

Schools of Illumination. Parts 1-2.

Lond. 1914-1915, fol.

B.—BODLEIAN LIBRARY (see p. 97).

1. Catalogi librorum manuscriptorum Angliæ et
Hiberniæ in unum collecti cum indice alphabetico.

Oxoniæ, e Theatro Sheldoniano, 1697, fol.

This is the ' Old Catalogue,' chiefly edited by Dr.
Edward Bernard. The 1st part of vol. i., about two-
fifths of the whole, deals with the MSS. in the
Bodleian ; part 2, MSS. in Oxford Colleges ; part
3, MSS. in some Cambridge Colleges and the
University Library ; vol. ii., part 1, catalogues
MSS. in Cathedral Libraries and private hands ;
part 2, Irish collections. Each part has a separate
index. The Bodleian collections here found, and
still not elsewhere fully described in print, are
those entitled, e Musæo, James, Fairfax, Hatton,
Leland, Junius, Marshall, Barlow, Dugdale, Wood,
and Fell. Unfortunately no indication of the age of
a MS. is given, but the work is by no means superseded.

(Catalogus codicum manuscriptorum Orientalium . . .
pars i. ; a J. Uri (Oxf. 1788, fol.) ; partis ii. vol. 1
ab A. Nicoll (Oxf. 1821, fol.) ; partis ii. vol. 2 ab
E. B. Pusey (Oxf. 1835, fol.).

2. Catalogus MSS. . . . E. D. Clarke . . . pars i.

(Oxf. 1812, 4to) ; pars 2 ab A. Nicoll (Oxf. 1814, 4to).

3. Catalogus codicum manuscriptorum et impressorum cum notis MSS. olim D'Orvillianorum . . . (Oxf. 1806, 4to).

4. Catalogus MSS. Borealium præcipue Islandicæ originis, a Finno Magnæo Islando (Oxf. 1832, 4to).

5. Catalogus codicum manuscriptorum Bibliothecæ Bodleianæ (' The Quarto Series ') :

Pars   i. Codices Græci, ab H. O. Coxe (Oxf. 1853, 4to). This includes also the Adversaria of Casaubon, Grabe, Langbaine, and St. Amand.

,,   ii. Codices Laudiani, ab H. O. Coxe, 2 fasciculi (Oxf. 1858-85, 4to).

,,   iii. Codices Græci et Latini Canoniciani, ab H. O. Coxe (Oxf. 1854, 4to).

,,   iv. Codices T. Tanneri, ab A. Hackman (Oxf. 1860, 4to).

,,   v. Codicum R. Rawlinson (fasc. 1) classes duæ priores, (fasc. 2) classis tertia cum indice trium classium, (fasc. 3-5) classis quarta cum indice, a Gul. D. Macray (Oxf. 1862-1900, 4to.)

,,   vi. (Syriac, 1864.)

,,   vii. (Aethiopic, 1848.)

,,   viii. (Sanskrit, 1859-1905.)

,,   ix. Codices Digbeiani, a Gul. D. Macray (Oxf. 1883, 4to.)

,,   x. Catalogue of the manuscripts bequeathed to the University by Elias Ashmole. By W. H. Black, with index by W. D. Macray (Oxf. 1845-67, 4to).

,,   xi. Catalogo di codici MSS. Canoniciani Italici, compilato dal Conte A. Mortara (Oxf. 1864, 4to).

,,   xii. (Hebrew, 1886-1906.)

„   xiii. (Persian, Turkish, Hindustani, Pushtu, part 1, 1889.)

,,   xiv. (Armenian, 1918.)

6. Calendar of the Clarendon State Papers, vols. 1-3,
   1523-1657. By O. Ogle, W. H. Bliss, and W. D.
   Macray (Oxf. 1869-76, 8vo : in progress).
   Manuscripts are also catalogued in the Gough (1841),
   Malone (1835), and Douce (1840) catalogues, in
   W.H. Turner's Calendar of Charters and Rolls (1878),
   and in minor books which cannot be here enumerated.
7. Summary Catalogue of Western MSS. not in the
   Quarto Series of Catalogues, vols. 2, part 1 ; 3-6, part
   2, by F. Madan (Oxf. 1905-20, 8vo : in progress)·
   Also Malay (1910) : Prakrit (1911) : Early Bodleian
   Music, by Sir J. Stainer and E. W. B. Nicholson, 3
   vols. (unofficial), 1901-13, fol.

C.—CAMBRIDGE UNIVERSITY LIBRARY (see p. 100).

Catalogue of the manuscripts (non-Oriental, but
including printed books with manuscript notes,
with indexes), 7 vols. (i.-v., index, adversaria),
Camb. 1856-67, 8vo.
(Also Hebrew, 1876 : Sanskrit, 1883 : Persian,
1896 : Muhammedan, 1900 : Syriac, 1901 : etc.)

D.—COLLEGE LIBRARIES OF OXFORD AND CAMBRIDGE.

1. *Oxford.*

Catalogus codicum manuscriptorum qui in Collegiis
Aulisque Oxoniensibus hodie adservantur. Confecit
H. O. Coxe (2 vols. : Oxf. 1852, 4to).
   This catalogue omits the Christ Church and Pem-
broke manuscripts. A supplement to the Corpus
Catalogue was issued in 1887. Some copies omit
the All Souls' MSS.
Catalogus codicum MSS. qui in bibliotheca Aedis

Christi apud Oxonienses adservantur. Curavit
G. W. Kitchin (Oxf. 1867, 4to).
    The MSS. both of the Chapter and of the House
    are included. For Pembroke College, Haenel's
    Catalogi librorum manuscriptorum (Leipzig, 1830,
    4to) must still be used.

2. Cambridge.

Catalogus librorum manuscriptorum quos Collegio
    Corporis Christi legavit Matthæus Parker archie-
    piscopus Cantuariensis.   Edidit Jacobus Nasmyth
    (Camb. 1777, 4to).
The present Provost of Eton College (Dr. M. R.
    James) has provided a fine set of Catalogues of the
    MSS. of the following Colleges :—Christ's, Clare,
    Corpus, Emmanuel, Gonville and Caius, Jesus,
    King's, Magdalene, Pembroke, Peterhouse, Queens',
    St. John's, Sidney Sussex, Trinity, Trinity Hall,
    and of the Fitzwilliam Museum.   They have been
    issued between 1895 and 1914.

E.—Phillipps Library.

Catalogus librorum manuscriptorum in bibliotheca D.
    Thomæ Phillipps, Bart. (Middlehill and Chelten-
    ham, 1837-(71), fol.) ; this comprises MSS. 1 to
    about 30,000, with rough indexes to MSS. 1-11,506
    only.   Not published, and unfinished, but accessible
    in large libraries.   The first 3000 or so are in
    Haenel's *Catalogi*, as above).   Since 1886 this
    magnificent library has been sold piecemeal by
    auction and otherwise, but much still remains to
    be dispersed.   See p. 101.

APPENDIX C.

BOOKS USEFUL FOR THE STUDY OF MANUSCRIPTS.

(The titles are not in all cases taken from the books themselves, but are sufficiently accurate for the present purpose. Expensive works are marked with an asterisk at the beginning of the title, and those which can be obtained for less than 10s. by an asterisk at the end. The lists within each section are arranged to some extent in order of present utility, but are by no means complete.)

1. OLD WRITING IN GENERAL.

Introduction to Greek and Latin Palæography, by Sir E. Maunde Thompson, 1912, 8vo.

Encyclopædia Britannica, art. Palæography, by Sir E. Maunde Thompson, 1911, 4to.

Berger, P. ; Histoire de' l'Écriture dans l'antiquité, 2nd ed. 1892, 4to.

Silvestre, J. B. : Historical and descriptive text and introduction to his *Universal Palæography*, by Champollion-Figeac and Aimé Champollion, translated and edited by Sir F. Madden, 2 vols. 1849, 8vo.

Taylor, Isaac : The Alphabet, 2 vols. 1899, 8vo.

The only first-rate book on musical neums and notes is the late H. M. Bannister's. * Monumenti Vaticani di paleografia musicale Latina, 1913, fol.

(*a*) *Greek Writing.*

Gardthausen, V. ; Griechische Paläographie, 1911, 8vo.

Kenyon, Sir F. G. : Palæography of Greek Papyri, 1899, 8vo.

Montfaucon, Bern. : Palæographia Græca, 1708, fol.   The old and classical work on the subject, with facsimiles.

Wattenbach, W. : Anleitung zur griechischen Paläographie,* 3rd ed. 1895, 4to, with separate facsimiles.

(*b*) *Latin Writing.*

Reusens, E. H. J. : Éléments de Paléographie, 1897-9, 8vo.

Prou, M. : Manuel de Paléographie, latine et française, 1910, 8vo.

Chassant, Alphonse : Dictionnaire des Abréviations,* 5th ed. 1884, 8vo.   This deals with Latin and French.

Cappelli, A. : Dizionario di Abbreviature,* 1912, 8vo.

Wattenbach, W. : Anleitung zur lateinischen Paläographie,* 1886, 4to.

The old classical works on the subject, not really superseded, are Mabillon's De Re Diplomatica libri vi., 1681 or 1709, fol., with supplement, 1704, fol. ; or 1789, 2 vols. fol.; with facsimiles : (Toustain and Tassin's)* Nouveau Traité de Diplomatique, 6 vols. 1750-65, 4to, with facsimiles ; and Kopp's Tachygraphia veterum, 2 vols. 1817, 4to, especially dealing with Latin shorthand (Tironian notes).

For Latin contractions, besides Chassant and Cappelli above, Walther's Lexicon Diplomaticum, 1745-47, or 1752, or 1756, fol. ; C. Trice Martin's Record Interpreter, 1892, 8vo ; and lists in vol. iv. of the Registrum Palatinum Dunelmense (Rolls series), 1878, 8vo, and vol. iii. of the Pipe Roll Society's publications, 1884, 8vo, may be used. And for mediæval Latin, * Du Cange's Glossarium ad Scriptores mediæ et infimæ Latinitatis (best ed. 10 vols. 1883-87, 4to), or Maigne d'Arnis's one volume abridgment fo it (1866, 8vo), are the best books ; and for English law terms in Latin, Norman-French, or English, Cowell's Law Dictionary (best ed. 1727, fol.).

(c) *English Writing.*

Thompson, Sir E. Maunde : History of English Handwriting, 1899-1901, 8vo.

For old English legal deeds in Court-hand, whether in Latin or English, there is Johnson and Jenkinson's English Court-hand, 1066-1500, 2 vols., 1915, 8vo and fol., and C. Trice Martin's ed. of Wright's Court-hand Restored, 9th ed. 1879, 4to, with facsimiles. Madox's Formulare Anglicanum (Lond. 1702, fol.) gives numberless specimens of deeds of all kinds. Giry's Manuel de Diplomatique, 1894, 8vo, is a standard work.

2. SCRIBES AND THE PRODUCTION OF BOOKS.

Birt, Theodor : Das antike Buchwesen, 1882, 8vo : Die Buchrolle in der Kunst, 1907, 8vo.

Wattenbach, W. : Das Schriftwesen im Mittelalter, 2nd ed. 1875, 8vo.

Sir Thomas Duffus Hardy's Introduction in the third volume of his Descriptive Catalogue of Materials relating to the History of Great Britain and Ireland (Rolls series), 1871, 8vo : Richard de Bury's Philobiblon, the first book on the love of books, finished in $134\frac{4}{5}$ (best ed. by Prof. A. F. West for the Grolier Club at New York, 3 vols. 1889, sm. 4to ; next best by E. C. Thomas,* Lond. 1888, 8vo) ; F. S. Merry-weather's Bibliomania in the Middle Ages,* 1849, 8vo ; Isaac Taylor's History of the Transmission of Ancient Books to Modern Times,* 1875, 8vo ; and S. R. Maitland's Dark Ages, 2nd ed. 1845, 8vo, may still be consulted.

Mr. F. W. Hall's Companion to Classical Texts (1913, 8vo) contains much about Textual Criticism, and there is a small but excellent manual of Latin Textual Emendation* by Prof. W. M. Lindsay (1896, 8vo), but many good treatises on Textual Criticism are chiefly con-cerned with the study of the New Testament, such as Westcott and Hort's Introduction to their edition of the New Testament (1881), Kenyon's Textual Criticism of the N. T. (1901) ; Kirsopp Lake's Text of the New Testament,* 1902, 12mo. J. N. Madvig's De Arte Coniecturali in vol. i. of his Adversaria Critica (1871) is of value. Ludwig Traube's various works are full of the subject.

3. ILLUMINATIONS AND FACSIMILES.

(a) *Works on Illuminations.*

Herbert, J. A. : Illuminated Manuscripts, 1911,
8vo. This is the best work on the subject.

Thompson, Sir E. Maunde : English Illuminated
Manuscripts, 1895, 8vo.

Tymms, W. R., and M. D. Wyatt : The Art of
Illuminating, 1860, 4to.

Bradley, J. W. : A Dictionary of Miniaturists,
3 vols. 1887-89, 8vo.

Shaw, Henry : The Art of Illumination, 1870,
4to.

Birch, W. de G., and H. Jenner : Early
Drawings and Illuminations in the British
Museum, 1879, 8vo ; a long list arranged by
subjects, with introduction.

Mrs. Merrifield collected and edited several
old treatises on the technical side of illumination (2 vols. 1849, 8vo).

(b) *Works chiefly consisting of coloured Facsimiles of
Illuminations.*

*Bastard, Count P. Auguste de : Peintures et
Ornements des Manuscrits, 1835-83, fol. This
is the finest work on illuminations in existence, but is far beyond the means of ordinary
students. Special copies have special additions.

*Silvestre, J. B. : Universal Palæography, or
Facsimiles of Writings of all nations and
periods, translated and edited by Sir F.
Madden, 2 vols. 1850, fol. See above, p. 195.

A selection entitled *Palæographical Album*, with 72 plates, was also issued.

*Westwood, J. O.: Palæographia Sacra Pictoria, n.d. 4to, with descriptions of fine illuminated Biblical MSS. in many languages.

*—— Illuminated Illustrations of the Bible, 1846, 4to.

*—— Miniatures and Ornaments of Anglo-Saxon and Irish Manuscripts, 1868, fol.: a splendid work, and accompanied by valuable descriptions of the manuscripts.

Shaw, Henry: Illuminated Ornaments selected from Manuscripts and early printed books, 1833, fol.

See also British Museum Catalogues (p. 190).

(c) *Works chiefly consisting of uncoloured Facsimiles of Writing and Illumination.* (See also the list of British Museum Catalogues, above, p. 189, etc.).

*The Palæographical Society's publications, 1873, etc., fol.

*The New Palæographical Society's publications, 1903, etc., fol.

Works by Leopold Delisle and Henri Omont.

————

Wattenbach, W., and A. von Velsen: Exempla codicum Græcorum litteris minusculis scriptorum, 1878, 4to.

Zangemeister, C., and W. Wattenbach: Exempla codicum Latinorum litteris maiusculis scriptorum, 1876-79, 4to.

Arndt, W.: Schrift-tafeln (Latin), 1903-6, fol.

Appendix C

Delisle, Leopold : Le Cabinet des Manuscrits de la Bibliothèque Nationale (4 quarto volumes, 1868-81).

Ellis, Robinson : Facsimiles from Latin MSS. in the Bodleian Library, 2 series, 1885-91, 4to. The series contains 12 and 20 plates respectively.

Steffens, F. : Lat. Paläographie, 1909, fol.

---

*Facsimiles of National Manuscripts of England (4 vols. 1865-68, 4to), Ireland (4 vols. in 5, 1874-84, 4to), and Scotland (3 vols. 1867-71, 4to).

*Facsimiles of Anglo-Saxon Charters, 1873-8 (4 vols., 4to and fol.).

Skeat, Prof. W. W. : Twelve Facsimiles of Old English Manuscripts,* 1892, 4to.

Appendix to Reports from the Commissioners on the Public Records (1820), fol. 86 plates from the Public Records.

For the study of autographs, the best book is Scott and Davey's Guide to the Collector of Historical Documents, 1891, 4to ; which contains a careful index to printed sets of Facsimiles of autographs in 143 printed works, and includes a reproduction of part of Wright's Court-hand Restored. See also W. J. Hardy's Handwriting of the Kings and Queens of England (1893, large 8vo).

4. Libraries and Collectors.

> Encyclopædia Britannica, art. Libraries, by H. R.
> Tedder, 1911, 4to. This contains a valuable
> bibliography, which could be supplemented by
> consulting the American Library Journal, the
> Journal of the Library Association of the United
> Kingdom) at present the *Library Association
> Record*) and *Minerva*.
>
> Edwards, Edward : Memoirs of Libraries, 2 vols.
> 1859, 8vo : vol. i. of a second edition was issued.
> —— Libraries and Founders of Libraries, 1864,
> 8vo.
>
> The fourth book of Edwards's Free Town Libraries
> (1869, 8vo) is ' Historical Notices of Book Col-
> lectors,' and the late Bernard Quaritch started a
> valuable collection of similar notes ; see also
> Elton's volume in the first edition of this series.
>
> Clark, J. Willis : The Care of Books, 1909, 8vo.
> A valuable historical work.
>
> Becker, G. : Catalogi bibliothecarum antiqui,
> 1885, 8vo.
>
> Gottlieb, T. : Ueber mittelalterliche Bibliotheken,
> 1890, 8vo.
>
> Savage, E. A., and J. Hutt : Old English Libraries,
> 1911, 8vo.

5. Records.

> Sims, Richard : A Manual for the genealogist (the
> three issues from 1861 on are practically
> identical).

Phillimore, W. P. W. : How to write the History
of a Family,* 2nd ed., 1888, 8vo, with the 2nd
ed. of the Supplement (1900).

Rye, Walter : Records and Record Searching,*
1888, 8vo.

Cox, J. C. : How to write the History of a Parish,*
1879, 8vo.

Scargill-Bird, S. R. : A Guide to the Public Record
Office, 3rd ed. (1908, 8vo).

Thoyts, E. E. (now Mrs. Cope) : How to Decipher
Old Documents,* 1909, 8vo.

INDEX

ABBREVIATION and Contraction, 33-39.
Acton, Lord, 100.
Æthelwold, Benedictional of, 102.
Alcuin, 29, 31, 62 ; his Bible, 116.
Alexandria, 88.
Alexandrinus, Codex, 82.
Alphabet, history of the, 21.
Anglo-Saxon Chronicle, 118.
Apostolic Canons and Constitutions, 132.
Archetype, 69.
Aristotle, 110.
Armarius, 43, cf. 90.
Arrian, 69.
Arundel MSS., 96, App. B.
Ashburnham MSS., App. B.
Ashmolean Museum at Oxford, 22, 99, 106, App. B.
Augustine Gospels, 30.
Autographs, 143.

BARK, writing on, 7.
Barocci MSS., 98.
Bedford Hours, *see* Plate II. description.
Benedictines, 41, 43, 57, 89.
Benedictional of Æthelwold, 102.
Beneventan, 28.
Bentley, Dr. Richard, 131.
Beowulf, 119.
Beza, Theodorus, 83.
Bible, the word, 10 ; Biblical MSS., 63, 82, 111, 117 ; Old Testament, 49, 60, 86, 111, 125, 126 ; New Testament, 49, 86, 114, 115 : etc.

Binding, 48, 160.
Bodleian Library at Oxford, account of, 97 ; MSS., App. A, B ; (Arrian), 69 ; (Augustine Gospels), 30 ; (Caedmon), 120 ; (Laudian Chronicle), 118 ; (St. Margaret's Gospel-Book), 122 ;(Ormesby Psalter), 64 ; catalogues, App. B.
Bodley, Sir Thomas, 97.
Book, the word, 7 ; *see* chap. i.
Book-hand, 26.
Books on writing, etc., *see* App. C.
Book-worms, 161.
Borders, illuminated, 64.
Boustrophedon, 140.
Boyle and Bentley controversy, 130.
Breviary, 154.
British Museum in London, account of, 93 ; collections, 94 ; MSS., App. A, B ; (Beowulf), 119 ; (clay tablets), 88 ; (Codex Alexandrinus), 82 ; (Cottonian Genesis), 111 ; (Dunstan Charter), 148 ; Hyperides), 110 ; (Ingulphus) 134 ; (Melissenda Psalter), 49 ; (Old English Chronicle), 118 ; (double palimpsest), 81 ; (Arundel and Queen Mary's Psalters, 64) ; (Lindisfarne Gospels), 117 ; 81, 117, 135 ; catalogues, App. B.
Bruni, Leonardo, of Arezzo, 147.

Index 205

Bulls, Pontifical, 13.
Burney MSS., 96, App. B.
Bury, Bp. Richard de, 91.
Byzantine ornamentation, 60, 62.

CADMUS, legend of, 23.
Cacdmon, 120 ; Plate VIII. description.
Cambridge University Library, account of, 100 ; MSS., 64, App. A.; (Codex Bezæ), 83 ; College MSS., 101, App. B; (Corpus), 118 ; catalogues, App. B.
Canonici MSS., App. B.
Canons of criticism, 74.
Canterbury MSS., 149, 159.
Capitals, 27 ; similarity of ancient and modern, 27.
Capsa, 90.
Carolingian minuscule, 28, 31.
Carte papers, 99.
Casket Letters, 150.
Cataloguing MSS., 162.
Cathach Psalter, 61.
Celt, 84.
Chained books, 90.
Chain-lines, 17.
Chalcis in Eubœa, 24.
Charles the Great, 28, 32, 62.
Charta, 9 ; bombycina, 12.
Chasles, —., 144.
Chatterton, Thomas, 135.
Clarendon papers, 99, App. B.
Clark, A. C., 75.
Clay tablets, 14, 88.
Close rolls, 170.
Codex, 7.
Collectors' weaknesses, 164.
Collier, John Payne, 138.
Colophons, 48 ; examples of, 54.
Colours in illumination, 57.
Columba, St., 30, 50.
Columns in a page, 10.
Conjectural emendation, 71.
Constantine, Donation of, 150.
Contractions, 33-39.
Corrector, 48.

Cotton, Sir Robert Bruce, 104 ; his MSS., 94, App. B ; injury to them by fire, 111.
Court-hand, 26, 33.
Court rolls, 177.
Cromwell MSS., 98.
Croyland, history of, 134.
Cumæ, 24.
Curiosities of palæography, 84.
Cursive, 25.
Cuthbert, St., 49.

D, history of the letter, 24.
Date, mode of expressing a, (20 June 1379), 175.
Dating MSS., 158.
Decretals, the False, 132.
Deeds, kinds of, 173.
Devonshire, Duke of, 102.
Dictare, 40.
Dictation, 40.
Digby MSS., 98, App. B.
Dodsworth MSS., 99.
Domesday book, 168.
Donation of Constantine, 150.
Douce MSS., 99.
Dublin, Trinity College, 61, 101.
Dunstan's supposed writing, 148.
Durrow, book of, 101.

EAST ANGLIAN Illumination, 63.
Ebesham, William, 52.
Ecclesiastical records, 172.
Egyptian writing, 22 ; schoolboy's letter, 110.
Εἰκὼν Βασιλική, 151.
English, alphabet, 21 ; writing and illumination, 30, 63 ; *see also Hiberno-Saxon*, Plates V., VIII.
Enurchus, St., 85.
Ephraëmi Codex, 83.
Epic Cycle, 47.
Epictetus, 69.
Essonia, 179.
Et (ampersand), 20.
Evolvere, 10.

Exemplification, 175.
Exeter MSS., 98.
Explicit, 10.

FAIRFAX MSS., 98.
False Decretals, 132.
Florence MSS., 80, App. A.
Foliating MSS., 162.
Folio, meaning, 15.
Forgeries, *see* chap. ix.
French writing and illumina-
    tion, 31, 64.   Plates II., VI.

GELLIUS, Aulus, 80.
Genealogy in MSS., 69, 78.
German writing and illumina-
    tion, 31, 63, 66.
Ghost-words, 84.
Glanville, Bartholomæus, 13.
Glosses, 73.
Gloucester, Humphrey, Duke
    of, 97.
Gold in MSS., 58.
Gospels, history of the four,
    81 ; *see* also *Bible*.
Gothic, hand, 31.
Gough MSS., 85.
Greek, 23 ; MSS., 82, 108.

HALF-UNCIAL writing, 27.
Hargrave MSS., 96, App. B.
Harleian MSS., 94, 95, App. B.
Henry VII., date of birth, 126.
Heraldic visitations, 177.
Herculanean rolls, 89, 109.
Hiberno-Saxon, 30, 31.
Hieratic, 22, 24.
Hieroglyphic, 22, 24. Plate VII.
Hispana, 133.
Historiographus, 41.
Homer, 47.
Homoioteleuton, 72.
Horæ (Book of Hours), 155.
Hundred rolls, 171.
Huntington MSS., 99, 106.
Hyperides, 8, 110.

IDEOGRAMS, 19.

Illuminations, cost of, 51, 52 ;
    colours used in, 57 ; in
    liturgical MSS., 155 ; how
    to describe, 163 ; *see* Chap.
    V., App. C.
Illuminatores, 44, 57.
Incipit, 10.
Indentures, 176.
Ingulphus, 134.
Inquisitions, 171.
Ink, 17.
Inspeximus, 175.
Insular, 30, 31.
Iona, 30.
Ireland and Irish writing and
    illumination, 29, 61, 114 ; *see*
    also *Hiberno-Saxon*, descrip-
    tion of Frontispiece.
Ireland, W. H., 137.
Isidorus Mercator, 133.
Italian writing and illumina-
    tion, 32, 66.

JERVAULX abbey, 86.
Johnson, Dr. Samuel, 137.

KELLS, book of, 61 ; account
    of, 114 ; *see* Frontispiece.
Knights' fees, 169.

LANSDOWNE MSS., 96, App. B.
Latin, 2, 108.
Laudian MSS., 98, App. B.
Laugharne, 86.
Leipzig, MS. at, 112.
Leonardus Aretinus, 147.
Liber, 7.
Libraries, *see* Chap. VII., App.
    A (statistics), B (catalogues),
    C (books on them)
Librarii, 44.
Libri, Guillaume, 104.
Licinianus, C. Granius, 81.
Lindisfarne, 30, 115.
Liturgical MSS., 153-7.
Localization, 44, 159.
London : *see* British Museum.
Lucar, Cyril, 82.
Lyons, 83.

M, history of the letter, 24.
Majuscule, 26.
Manchester, John Rylands library, 49, App. A.
Manuscripts, *see* List of Contents ; meaning of word, 1 ; use of study of, *introdn.* ; rights of ownership of, 104 ; statistics of European, App. A.
Margaret, St., Queen of Scotland, 122.
Marsh MSS., 99.
Martial, 40, 50.
Mary Queen of Scots, 150.
Melissenda, 49.
Merovingian, 28.
Mielot, Jean ; *see* Plate IV., description.
Milan, Ambrosian MSS. at, 59, App. A.
Minuscule, 26.
Miracle, MS. the subject of a, 123.
Missal, 154.
Mixture in MSS., 71.
Moabite Stone, 22.
Moore library, 100.

NAPLES, MSS. at, 89, 109, App. A. ; liturgy of, 115.
National hands, 26, 28.
Nicene Creed on silver, 6.
Nineveh, 88.
Noster, 35.
Notarii, 41, 44.

OCTAVO, meaning, 16.
Omar, Caliph, 88.
Ossian, 151.
Ostraka, 14.
Ownership, 104.
Oxford, *see Ashmolean Museum, Bodleian Library :* College MSS., 101, App. B ; (Exeter), 125 ; (Queen's), 102.
Oxford, Robert and Edward, Earls of, 95.

PALÆOGRAPHY, use of study, *introdn.* ; *see Manuscripts.*
Palimpsests, 81.
Paper, the word, 9 ; as material, 12, 13, 15.
Papyri, remarkable, 107.
Papyrus, 7, 12.
Parchment, 11, 13.
Parian Chronicle, 6.
Paris National Library, 60, 83, 103, 107, App. A.
Paris, Matthew, 42, 44.
Parker MSS., 101.
Paston Letters, 52, 126.
Patent rolls, 170.
Pedes finium, 171.
Pens, 17.
Pergamena, 11.
Perrins, H. Dyson, 64, 103.
Petrograd (Codex Sinaiticus), 82, 111, 142, App. A.
Phalaris, letters of, 130.
Phillipps Library, 101, 140, App. B.
Phœnician, 22.
Phonographic writing, 20.
Photography for MSS., 105, 165.
Picture writing, 19, 20.
Pipe rolls, 170.
Placita de quo warranto, 171.
Pococke MSS., 99.
Poggio Bracciolini, 145.
Pompeii, 18, 109.
Portiforium, 157.
Prices of writing, etc., 51.
Primer, 157.
Printing, source of modern, 32.
Prisse papyrus, 107.
Procopius, 147.
Prust, John, 51.
Purple MSS., 58.

QUARITCH, Bernard, 102.
Quarto, meaning, 16.
Quaternions, 15.
" Queen Mary's Psalter," 64.
Quire, 15.

RAWLINSON MSS., 99, App. B.
Records in England, 167.
Registers, parish, 173.
Reynbold, John, 51.
Richard de Bury, Bp., 91.
Roll-form of book, 14.
Rome, 89; see Vatican;
    liturgy of, 116.
Rosetta stone, 6.
Rowley, Thomas, 136.
Royal collections of MSS., 94,
    App. B.
Rubricator, 48.
Ruling of MSS., 45.
Rustic capitals, 27, 81.

SACRAMENTARY, 157; see Plate
    III.
St. Alban's, 42, 44, 45.
St. Gall, 27, 81.
Samarkand, 13.
Sarum, 87.
Scipios, tombs of the, 6.
Scribes, see Chaps. IV., VI.
Scriptorium, 41, 42; see Plate
    IV.
Section of a book, 15.
Selden MSS., 99.
Semitic, Old, 21.
Send or Sent inscription, 22,
    106, Plate VII.
Servatus Lupus, 70.
Shakespeare forgeries, 137.
Shapira, 143.
Siatoutanda, 147.
Signatures in books, 160.
Signatures of witnesses, 176.
Siloam inscription, 22.
Silver in MSS., 58.
Simonides, Constantine, 139.
Sinaiticus, Codex, 82, 111, 142.
Size of MSS., 14-15.
Sloane MSS., 95, App. B.
Spain, paper in, 13.
Stilus, 13.
Stone inscriptions, 6.
Stonyhurst, MS. Gospel at, 49.
Stowe, missal, 50; MSS., 97,
    App. B.

Suspension, 34, 36.
Syriac, 97, 111.

TACITUS, 145.
Tanner MSS., 99, App. B.
Te Deum, 85.
Ten Commandments, 6.
Terence, 60.
Textual criticism, see Chap. VI.
Theca, 49.
Thompson, H. Yates, 103.
Thucydides, 129.
Timotheus, 108.
Tischendorf, Constantine, 111
Titchfield Abbey library, 91.
Tours, 29, 31.
Traube, L., 33, 70.

ULFILAS, 82.
Uncial writing, 27.
Uranius, 140.
Ussher MSS., 101, 114.
Utrecht Psalter, 104.

VALERIUS Maximus, 70.
Vatican Library, 59, 60, 80,
    82, 103, App. A.
Vellum, 11.
Venice, MSS. at, App. A.
Verona, MS. at, 80.
Vesuvius, 89, 109.
Vienna, MS. at, 108.
Virgil, manuscripts of, 27,
    59; examples of errors from
    MSS. of Virgil, 74, cf. 86;
    literary history of, 79.
Visigothic, 28.
Visitations, heraldic, 177.
Volume, the word, 10.
Vrain-Lucas forgeries, 143.

WALPOLE, Horace, 137.
Watermarks, 13, 16
Wax tablets, 108.
Whitby, 120; council of, 30.
Windsor MSS., 98.
Wills, 176.
Writing, history of, see Chaps.
    II., III., IV., App. C.;
    details of scribe's work, 45.
Wood, writing on, 7.

PRINTED BY THE ANCHOR PRESS, LTD., TIPTREE, ESSEX, ENGLAND